THE GROWING CHURCH

THE GROWING CHURCH

Keys to Congregational Vitality

Thom Belote, Editor

SKINNER HOUSE BOOKS
BOSTON

Published by Skinner House Books, an imprint of the Unitarian Universalist Association of Congregations, a liberal religious organization with more than 1,000 congregations in the U.S. and Canada, 25 Beacon St., Boston, MA 02108-2800.

Printed in the United States

Cover and text design by Suzanne Morgan
Cover art *Quincunx 1*, © 2004 Tracey Adams, www.traceyadamsart.com/

ISBN 1-55896-559-9
978-1-55896-559-1

13 12 11 10
6 5 4 3 2 1

Library of Congress Cataloging-in-Publication Data

The growing church : keys to congregational vitality / Thom Belote, editor.
p. cm.
ISBN-13: 978-1-55896-559-1 (pbk. : alk. paper)
ISBN-10: 1-55896-559-9 (pbk. : alk. paper)
1. Church growth. 2. Unitarian Universalist Association—Doctrines.
3. Unitarian Universalist churches—Doctrines. I. Belote, Thom.
BV652.25.G728 2010
254'.5—dc22
                                    2009029771

CONTENTS

FOREWORD

These essays continue a conversation that began a couple years ago when I joined the authors in Louisville, Kentucky, for a series of discussions about how their congregations have grown in spirituality, membership, and mission. As ministers of some of the fastest-growing Unitarian Universalist congregations, their success stories and insights are well worth sharing.

Reading their remarks, I feel hopeful for the enterprise we often call *church*. I feel a sense of pride, to be identified even distantly with these exemplary spiritual leaders. And, perhaps most powerfully, I feel confirmed and encouraged in my own sense of calling. Associating with this circle of colleagues has evoked—rather unexpectedly— a renewal of vows to seek and serve the holy in all of life.

I joined this circle in an unusual and privileged role. Not as a teacher or a keynote speaker. Not as the process designer, since a splendid format for the conversation had already been selected when the event was planned. Not even as the primary facilitator—once we had all made a commitment to hold the space open in a particular way, the circle guided itself. In retrospect, I realize that I was called there to witness this conversation on behalf of faith communities everywhere, and to honor the deep intentions to listen and to learn that had given birth to the conversation in the first place.

The whole event was a process of paying attention together, through the powerful lens of the wisdom circle—an instrument made not of glass but of our bodies and minds, and of the open spaces between and beyond us, connected in a sacred geometry. Through that lens, we examined the work of twelve people whose ministries have been especially fruitful over time. Participating in this conversation, and then continuing it in this volume, are profoundly counter-cultural moves. These ministers:

- ❖ Take a stand about what constitutes fruitful ministry, not by presenting a dry list of statements but by identifying living examples of the spiritual leadership they hope to foster.

- ❖ Give higher value to the long-term trajectory of their leadership than to flashy projects or quick results.

- ❖ Set aside the problematic narrative of mainline Protestant decline in favor of appreciative and honest inquiry.

- ❖ Create a supportive setting in which they can express their vision of ministry, describe critical moments and challenges, and share what they are learning.

- ❖ Adopt a posture of deep listening, allowing the words and lives of their colleagues to speak to them about the purpose and direction of their own leadership.

In Louisville, and in these pages, the authors have come together on holy ground. They have developed meaningful programs and thoughtful methods in their work, but these conversations focus persistently on the deeper calling we all share—ministers and members alike—to serve a gracious reality beyond ourselves, to notice the burning bushes all around us, to join the sacred dance of life and death.

Each essay opens a window onto some aspect of the conversation, and introducing us to the heart and mind of a fine leader. While the insights easily cross boundaries of location and denomination, the shape of the conversation itself may have the most powerful and portable implications for faith communities. At a time when denominational bodies must radically rethink their role and function, the UUA has provided us with a dazzling glimpse of a different way for congregations to be connected and a different way for denominations to lead.

—Alice Mann
Senior Consultant, the Alban Institute

INTRODUCTION

Whenever Unitarian Universalist leaders gather to set priorities—
whether in individual congregations, clusters, or national gatherings
—growth always emerges as one of our most important goals.

During my recent tenure as its president, the Association of
Congregations experimented, looking for ways to encourage, inspire,
and support the growth of our congregations. We initiated regional
marketing, national advertising, the recognition of "breakthrough
congregations," and attempts at large church start-ups, and we supported innovative new programs by congregations. We produced
banners, billboards, and bumper stickers—and a surprising number
of our congregations used them.

We had some real successes and some disappointments. We
learned a great deal, but the national adult membership numbers
have been hard to budge. While national growth has been modest,
some of our congregations have experienced rapid growth.

Two years ago, the UUA's Growth Team called together a group
of ministers serving some of the fastest-growing Unitarian Universalist congregations in the United States. We asked them to share both
their analysis and their experience of what made that growth possible
and rewarding. We selected ministers serving congregations of different sizes and from every part of the country. Dynamics and issues
vary by congregational size, and the demographics and economic
realities of particular areas must be taken into account. But, unde-
niably, our message and our covenantal way of living in religious
community can support far more individuals and families than have
found us thus far. The consultation was videotaped and released as a
DVD called *Listening to Experience*.

In this volume, those ministers go deeper, telling the stories of their experiences in a more fulsome way and offering what they have learned in the hope of helping us all. Each author has chosen a facet of growth to lift up from his or her own ministry. Some essays deal with concrete ideas, such as how to make the message of your church relevant to the larger society and how to develop a mission statement. Some describe worship that touches the soul, ways to make a congregation more welcoming, and the importance of embracing innovation. Others are more abstract, considering the responsible use of power, the idea of devotion, the central importance of love, and the cultivation of that feeling of energy, spirit, charisma, and excitement known as "buzz."

As you read these essays, you will be struck by the ministers' distinct personalities. Some are deeply pastoral, some rigorously intellectual, and some passionately prophetic. Indeed, all of them are "stars." They are intelligent, well trained, highly skilled, compassionate, and committed. But that is the profile of the typical Unitarian Universalist minister. The facets of growth they write about point to the diversity of elements that can foster and support growth. That is appropriate, given our distaste for fundamentalism of any kind.

At the same time, powerful common themes stand out. I remember so well sitting in the outer circle at the consultation with the other Growth Team members, while the ministers in the inner circle answered the facilitator's questions. The first was, "What is the saving message of your congregation?" I found the question itself surprising, and it was so helpful to hear in the answers a core of consensus. The language varied from minister to minister, but each told a similar story. "My congregation nurtures the individual human spirit and helps individuals find their connection to the holy, however they may name it." "My congregation is called to work for justice, to help heal the wounded world." In fact, "Nurture your spirit. Help heal our world" became a kind of mantra that ran through the consultation, so the UUA used it as its national advertising tagline for a while.

Our community places a high value on individualism, and every one of the four hundred congregations I visited as president believes itself unique. We invest a great deal of energy in dealing with the differences in our beliefs and our religious practices. Humanists and theists, liberal Christians and pagans, atheists and agnostics all find a home in Unitarian Universalist congregations. This big theological tent poses real challenges for our ministry. However, by focusing less on our differences of belief and more on what our congregations do, we might break through some of the dynamics that hold us back.

Love also emerged as a powerful theme in the consultation. Owing to the revelation of widespread sexual abuse by clergy in recent years, religious communities, including our own, have focused on necessary boundaries between ministers and congregants. Do not think for a moment that I would encourage us to undo that work. It is critically important. But an unintended consequence may be that we have given up the ability to talk about the appropriate love that must exist between a minister and congregation if the ministry is to thrive. It is clear that these ministers love their congregations. I would also venture to guess that their congregations experience being loved. We would be healthier if we could use that word more often. "Love is the doctrine of this church," begins one of our most commonly used statements of covenant. "Standing on the Side of Love" is one of our most popular hymns.

Another theme discussed in a few of these essays relates to conflict. Often, a period of sustained growth is triggered by the call of a new minister, so it would be easy to attribute such growth to that individual's skills and brilliance. And often, but not always, the period of growth follows a period of turmoil and conflict in congregational life. Conflict and turmoil are usually signs of a broken relationship. When a congregation and its minister have moved out of right relationship, sometimes the best solution is the call of a new minister. But perhaps we would be better served by developing a greater capacity to manage and move through conflict, by redeeming relationships and re-covenanting in ways that allow an existing ministry to move forward.

This book is a wonderful resource. Individual essays can be read by a congregational board or ministers' association chapter, and used as the basis for authentic and honest conversation. Worship commit-tees, membership committees, and other leadership groups will find much of value in these pages. It is clear that, as a movement, we have not yet found a reliable recipe for growth, nor is one presented here. But there is inspiration and a way to focus on some of the central issues we need to address.

As you read and use this book, I hope you can remember why the focus on growth is so important. It's not important because our congregations need more pledging units to pay the mortgage. Growth is not critical because larger and stronger congregations can witness more effectively for our values in the world, as important as that is. Growth is important because tens of thousands of individuals and families "out there" yearn for a liberal religious home. It takes considerable courage to visit a congregation when you know no one. Our visitors come because they have an empty space in their lives that they long to fill. We are called to respond to their needs and desires with our very best. We are called to do no less.

My special thanks go to Thom Belote, one of the ministers who participated in the consultation, for his willingness to edit this vol-ume. Our community should be grateful to him and to all these authors for being willing to share their experience and help move us forward.

—William Sinkford
President, Unitarian Universalist Association of Congregations,
2001–2009

Transformation

MICHAEL A. SCHULER

The newcomer orientation program at the First Unitarian Society of Madison is always popular. Since the recent major expansion of our national landmark facility, we have offered eight sections of that class each year and, typically, they are fully subscribed.

Many of the registrants are initially introduced to our congregation and Unitarian Universalism through the Internet. Most have attended services a few times and, recognizing our distinctiveness, are eager to learn more. The willingness of these folks to commit to a five-night series seems to indicate more than casual interest in our community.

I usually conduct the second session of these orientations. At the outset, I ask participants to identify the faith tradition in which they participated when growing up. As one might expect in our neck of the woods (the upper Midwest), people of Lutheran and Roman Catholic backgrounds predominate, with a smattering of other mainline Protestants, and an occasional lapsed Jew thrown into the mix. Only occasionally do I encounter a birthright Unitarian Universalist in an orientation class.

During the thirty-odd years I've been meeting with these groups, I've noticed a subtle but discernable shift in the attitude of these "come-outers." As recently as two decades ago, many refugees from orthodoxy routinely expressed dissatisfaction, if not outright disdain, for their former faith. No small number felt victimized—emotionally injured or intellectually stunted—by the previous relationship. Only half-jokingly would they claim to be "in recovery." The bitter tone so prevalent in the recent past is far less evident today. Indifference rather than distress is now the presenting issue. Orientation class participants don't accuse conventional churches and synagogues of doing any real harm, but they do feel that the spiritual issues they are most concerned about are not being adequately addressed. As Rev. Arvid Straube writes in *Salted With Fire*, "Many of today's potential [UUs] . . . are not looking for a refuge from Methodism, but from secularism, hedonism and consumerism."

From 1988 to 2008, the First Unitarian Society of Madison's adult membership grew from 500 to over 1,500. In 2006, the congregation launched a capital campaign that raised well over six million dollars to build a new state-of-the-art "green" sanctuary. Fifteen times more than any previous campaign had generated, this amount exceeded our consultant's projections by over 40 percent.

We have enjoyed sustained success without significantly altering our approach to worship and enrichment. Newcomers to the First Unitarian Society won't find a youth-oriented alternative service or pop-style music performed by a rock band. The message from the pulpit is accessible but also substantive and well researched. In other words, we haven't really followed the high-tech, culturally accommodating formula that is said to have produced the megachurch phenomenon.

We have, however, made excellence our first priority, whether in music, liturgy, pastoral care, adult spiritual enrichment, community outreach, children's religious education, facilities, or general administration. Equally important, the worship and program staffs make an effort to address the issues our members and prospective members seem to be concerned about. That is to say, we strive to stay relevant.

A growing number of Americans feel disquieted and spiritually adrift. They sense that the assumptions undergirding our outwardly prosperous civilization have failed to produce the fulfillment we have been taught to expect.

What more could we want? Since the end of World War II, Americans have enjoyed an unparalleled degree of comfort and convenience. A tremendous array of entertainments is available to us twenty-four hours a day, twelve months of the year. Until recently, the nation's political leadership has made tax relief an entitlement and repeatedly reassured us that any alteration in or sacrifice of "the American way of life" is wholly unnecessary.

The culture at large continues to conjure a vision of the good life that appeals to our self-indulgent and acquisitive instincts. To test that claim, open your browser and punch in that phrase—"good life"—then note the images that appear. The screen will fill with images of people lolling by the seashore, drinking champagne, driving expensive sports cars, being pampered by masseurs, skiing, or skydiving. The good life is also identified with long-stemmed roses, diamond necklaces, wads of cash, impeccably furnished penthouses—all representations of over-the-top luxury and once-in-a-lifetime vacations.

But paradoxically, during the sixty-year period since the so-called Good War ended, opinion polls have shown a steady decline in American happiness. In 1945, surveys indicated that our citizens were the happiest in the world. Today, at least twenty-four nations report a higher happiness quotient than we do. For all our privileges, that all-important sense of inner satisfaction has lessened and, in many cases, now eludes us.

With its penetrating insight into our mental and emotional conditioning, Buddhism has coined an apt metaphor for what ails us: the "hungry ghost." Eager for happiness and the experience of true contentment, this benighted creature subsists on the deceptively thin fare our culture provides, easily appropriated pleasures that dull the cravings but do not satisfy them. The habit of happiness, beauty that is more than skin-deep, and caring, trustworthy relationships lie beyond the ghost's reach and are usually beyond its ken. It hasn't acquired the tools or the self-discipline to tap into these wellsprings of nourishment.

In the Chinese language, the words *pin* and *tan* look similar on the printed page. The first means "greed," and the second, "poverty." This, in a nutshell, is the dilemma of the hungry ghost. It is greedy for experiences and possessions to fill its emptiness, yet for all the effort the ghost expends, it still feels impoverished. The hungry ghost may compensate for its emptiness through the compulsive quest for pleasure and prestige but is unlikely to find in such pursuits an antidote for its chronic discontent. In fact, such striving as often as not produces a bumper crop of bitter fruit: envy, resentment, deprivation, and anger instead of the hoped-for happiness.

The promising road maps offered by our hard-won consumerist culture have too often led us down blind alleys or into cul-de-sacs. Novelty, excitement, sensory stimulation, and satiation are supplied in abundance, but in terms of what human beings truly want and need, the systems we have devised do not help us.

Moreover, the prevailing cultural ethos has had a profoundly deleterious effect on the larger social and ecological systems on which we all depend, as increasing numbers of Americans have begun to realize. Overconsumption, the celebration of excess, repeated sacrifice of the common good for private gain, a perverse taste for violence, and an unhealthy thirst for retribution are side effects of a civilization that has turned the individual pursuit of private self-interest and safety from a vice into a virtue.

As a consequence, too many of us have lost our connection to a sustainable life path that leads to treasures of perennial value: a beautiful and healthy earth home, human communities where all are well served and feel secure, work that makes a genuine contribution to the common good, and play that restores one's body and lifts one's spirits. "Living lightly on the earth with simple, joyful elegance" is how Green America characterized an alternative cultural vision, one that progressive faith communities can help their members realize.

A thorough reappraisal of our thinking and expectations is in order, because the connection between financial or material well-being and happiness has become tenuous. In fact, once people realize a relatively modest standard of living, they experience little further improvement in their mental and emotional life. What seems to make human beings reliably happy are not the evanescent good times that movie theaters, restaurants, and amusement parks provide but decent health, dependable relationships, personal integrity, altruistic service, feelings of belonging, a sense of calling, and the ability to savor the moment without regret or anxiety. Whether they consciously realize it or not, these are the fruits people hope to yield from their commitments and daily activities. A responsive faith community will make this life-affirming, life-preserving agenda its own and become a catalyst for a much-needed transformational process.

Many Americans assume that religious communities are programmed to handle issues related to metaphysics: addressing and/or settling questions about the mind of God, the mechanics of salvation, and prospects for the afterlife. No small number of people harbor concerns about such matters, and they appreciate any assistance and reassurance the church can provide. Nevertheless, many spiritual seekers also grapple with serious life issues this side of the grave and are anxious to deal with them in a practical yet meaningful manner. Among the questions now being asked are these:

"Materially I am so blessed, but why am I not as happy or as grateful as I think I ought to be?"

"I'm always busy and never seem to have enough time, but what am I really accomplishing? I wake up in the middle of the night feeling that much of what I do seems beside the point."

"Everybody says it's okay for the individual to pursue his or her self-interest and that competition is a healthy thing. But it feels like I'm being greedy and not promoting the spirit of community. Isn't interdependence just as important a principle?"

"I have this uncomfortable sensation of alienation and don't know how to achieve a sense of belonging. What's causing that and what can I do about it?"

"Too many of my interactions with others feel superficial and lacking in substance. Where can I find a safe place to share my thoughts and concerns with other serious-minded people?"

Like politics as usual, "religion as usual" doesn't hold its former appeal. Faith communities that stubbornly maintain their traditional focus and refuse to take seriously the foregoing questions, or that ignore the confusion and inner conflict affecting many members of the current generation are likely to find their credibility diminishing and their ranks thinning.

Men and women bring these concerns to the orientation and spiritual enrichment classes at First Unitarian Society because they have been disappointed with the response they've received at other venues, religious and secular. They hope that a liberal faith community might help them gain valuable insight and provide sensible guidance in their search for a more abundant life.

Spencer Burke, former pastor of a Southern California megachurch, argues in *A Heretic's Guide to Eternity* that many American churches have suffered serious attrition because they have continued to operate under an outmoded set of assumptions. According to Burke, among the mistakes more conventional faith communities make are these: placing undue emphasis on the hereafter at the expense of the here and now; trying to capitalize, however indirectly, on people's fear of death; an obsession with boundaries—who is saved and who is lost; dogmatism that demands full assent to a prefabricated set of answers; an antimaterial bias that keeps people at arm's length and alienated from the natural world.

The demographics do not look good for the churches Burke describes. The typical member is now, on average, twenty-five years older than the rest of the population. Moreover, those who have given up on organized religion entirely represent the fastest-growing segment of the U.S. population. Unless faith communities begin addressing the issues that the current crop of spiritual seekers care about, they will be hard-pressed to keep their pews occupied.

Burke thinks that America's declining denominations do a disservice not only to the spiritually famished but to the core Christian message as well. Jesus himself, by word and example, offered his followers a prescription for the "good life." But when the church preaches that the man "lived only to die," it "misses the essence of who Jesus was." He—like Socrates, Gautama Buddha, and Confucius—was a visionary who audaciously introduced the possibility of a transformed humanity.

Other acute observers concur with Burke's sober assessment of the religious scene. "We seem to be between a rock and a hard place," Richard Holloway, former bishop of Edinburgh complains in *Looking in the Distance*. Too often the choice for an earnest spiritual seeker is either to "opt back into the authoritarian children's home from which we have only recently escaped," or to wander aimlessly in the "atomized confusion of today's society," taking our cues from a culture that encourages gluttony but fails to nourish.

Those seeking something more than spiritual pabulum don't have a great deal to choose from, the late philosopher Robert Solomon laments in *Spirituality for the Skeptic*. His own discipline had become too academic and arcane to be of much benefit to ordinary men and women wrestling with core existential questions. But spirituality isn't the answer either. Too often it is something of a sham, something cheap, "something with enormous pretentions devoid of content. . . . Thus, even the most wacky New Age religions get to fill many hearts that might much better find their own fulfillment, if only they were encouraged to do so."

Spencer Burke resigned from a highly successful ministry because he thought that the church he knew so well, and to which he had dedicated significant time and energy, was hopelessly trapped in an old paradigm. Equipped with computers and the Internet, people have near-instantaneous access to information from a huge variety of sources. Having claimed the freedom to form their own opinions, many people find it hard to accept any particular faith tradition as a repository of irrefutable answers. Burke suggests that religion reposition itself as a "guardian of the great questions" and create communities of conversation, where people can seriously engage those questions.

Since cultures intermingle and interpenetrate continuously in our increasingly pluralistic environment, a religion that maintains an imperialistic stance and insists that it alone is right and that all other spiritual perspectives are wrong will find itself at a disadvantage. "Moving forward," Burke writes, "we must celebrate difference," exhibiting not only tolerance for other faiths but a willingness to learn from them.

Finally, Burke says, people yearn for resanctification of everyday life. Disappointed with materialistic values, men and women are eager to inject (or discover) a spiritual note in their work, recreation, family life, and community work. "The new spiritual impulse is holistic" and senses that "all of life is touched by God, not just the religious bits," Burke concludes.

The Jungian therapist and former Catholic cleric Thomas Moore makes a similar point in *Care of the Soul.* "There are two ways of thinking about church and religion," he writes. "One is that we go to church to be in the presence of the holy. The other is that the church teaches us directly and symbolically to see the sacred dimension of everyday life . . . and helps us to sustain mindfulness about the religion that is inherent in everything we do."

In our urbanized, overstimulated, and technology-centered culture, a great many of us suffer from a "reverence deficit," as the classicist Paul Woodruff might put it. Our free enterprise system has taught us to think in terms of resources, commodities, and exchange value, which may make sound economic sense but shrinks too many souls and spawns too many hungry ghosts. We long to regard the world around us, or at least certain aspects of it, with a renewed sense of admiration and awe. Curiously enough, after striving for the past several centuries for as much control as possible, we humans have once again become aware of the limits of our knowledge and, therefore, of the need to develop a sense of proportion and apply the brakes to our self-aggrandizing tendencies. Reverence and its corollary, humility, are increasingly in demand.

It's interesting how closely the criticisms and recommendations of Burke and the other commentators coincide with the strategy our own faith tradition has adopted. The inclusive, investigative, receptive, and holistic approach to religion and spirituality that typifies high-functioning and successful Unitarian Universalist congregations is precisely what the present moment demands.

Authoritarian, fear-based religion still pulls in multitudes but may well have peaked in America. Churches that keep people in thrall with a stale message of punishment and reward have lost the public's allegiance in much of the developed world, and their credibility is gradually diminishing in this country as well. The time is ripe for the honest, down-to-earth, life-affirming Unitarian Universalism faith, because so many people in our dysfunctional culture truly long to be "saved," although not necessarily in the metaphysical sense. They have grown weary of a life that feels shallow, tedious, and less meaningful.

Salvation has for some time been a vexed term for religious liberals, but it is relevant to this discussion. In her essay on this subject in her book *Amazing Grace*, Kathleen Norris notes that in the original Hebrew, it meant "to be rescued from danger." In ancient Greek, it meant "to be made well." Liberated from its orthodox associations, the concept of salvation becomes serviceable even to avowed secularists.

Who can doubt that the barren culture we have created—one in which so many fail to flourish—is dangerous? It has deprived us of the happiness that is both our hope and our birthright. Likewise, as people who have felt spiritually out of sorts for so long, we find ourselves searching for something more than another palliative—not just temporary relief, but a real cure for what ails us. In either case, the ultimate intention is to be "saved."

But for those whose aversion to traditional theological language is unusually strong, a synonym might serve just as well. "People are leaving the church because they want a *transforming* spirituality," Spencer Burke writes, one that produces a fresh perspective with the power to redeem lives that are woefully short on purpose, gladness, and meaning. The operative term here is *transformation*, a notion whose universality is underscored by Thich Nhat Hanh, the venerable Buddhist teacher, who writes in *Living Buddha, Living Christ*: "A Sangha (Buddhist community) is real if it moves in the direction of transformation" and helps its members develop lives of "greater understanding, love, solidity, and stillness."

My own experience tells me that significant numbers of down-to-earth but chronically dissatisfied people seek and long for a life of precisely this quality and with these characteristics. They are ready to move in a new direction but need steady guidance and a trustworthy community in which to ground themselves.

Faith communities exist to create the optimal conditions and an environment within which salvation on these terms might be realized. Individuals might be able to achieve the same results on their own through self-disciplined study, reflection, contemplation, and service. But for the vast majority, participation in a community of shared practice provides the support and motivation needed to sustain these efforts. As Richard Holloway points out, for all their defects, faith communities offer dependable opportunities for people to come together for serious spiritual and ethical investigation, for the purpose of developing fresh and liberating insights and of cultivating a lifestyle that is "well-balanced, well-tempered, and well-intended."

Transformation, then, is—initially at least—more about a shift in outlook than one of substance. One day we awaken to the world in our accustomed manner, but then something causes us to see it from a fresh perspective. If the reframing experience is powerful enough, we are likely, over time, to change our comportment, goals, and life agenda as well.

The Kingdom of God that Jesus spoke about wasn't so much a place as a potential, which could occur only when a critical tipping point had been reached and enough people had been "converted" to Jesus' own revolutionary perspective. *Convert* means to "turn around" or "turn one's attention to." The concept of conversion indicates that, again, point of view is the initial and key factor in a person's ambition to make meaningful and meliorating life changes.

Let me offer an example of the instrumental role a Unitarian Universalist faith community played in the transformation process. On the second weekend of 2009, in our three worship services, I focused on the neglected issue of criminal justice in the United States. I spoke at some length and with copious documentation of the abuses to which the nation's 2.5 million prisoners are routinely subjected. Ours, I observed, had become in recent decades one of the most punitive, cruel, and unforgiving corrections systems on the planet. The long-term consequences of our incarceration policies are extremely troubling, deeply degrading for both inmates and a callous culture that, for the most part, has abandoned both the principle and practice of rehabilitation.

To be honest, I felt a little awkward delivering this jeremiad just ten days into the New Year. Although I had incorporated a number of practical suggestions for individual and congregational engagement, the service was clearly sobering rather than uplifting.

In the fellowship periods that followed, I was gratified by the number of listeners who approached me, some with a catch in their throat, saying, "I had no idea," or "That was really hard to hear, but I'm glad you said it," or "Our congregation really needs to find ways to address this problem." Apparently, even the well-informed, socially aware members of the First Unitarian Society hadn't kept up with developments in the American corrections system. They were unaware that, in its eagerness to "fight crime," our judicial system had managed to imprison fully one percent of the U.S. adult population, with the percentage of African Americans, Latinos, and Amerindians behind bars significantly higher. People learned that day that the Guantánamo Bay military detention center (Gitmo) isn't the aberration from normal practice they had been led to believe. American prisons in general are overcrowded, abusive, and, as those who manage the system concede, nearly intolerable.

Like the War on Terror and fundamentalist religion, America's draconian criminal justice policies are sustained by a carefully cultivated public fear of an omnipresent menace: the ruthlessly violent felon. When people learn that less than 8 percent of U.S. inmates have been convicted of violent crimes, they are first incredulous, then indignant, and ultimately ashamed.

On that second weekend of January, at least some of my listeners experienced a conversion. Their "attention had been turned," and consequently, they were in a position to revisit and perhaps revise previous assumptions. I appreciate the limits of sermonic eloquence; for most in attendance that weekend, prison reform will continue to be a low priority. But for at least a few, this judicious use of the "prophetic pulpit" may well have initiated a process of transformation.

Many clergy are reluctant to broach serious social issues, assuming that people come to church to be comforted, not stirred up or disturbed. But a growing number of Americans are deeply concerned about the current cultural climate, have limited confidence in the media, and are ready to hear the sort of straight talk that can lead to an alternative vision.

The First Unitarian Society of Madison has for better than two decades presented a countercultural message and has seen our membership triple, our giving increase fivefold, and our stature in the larger community rise to new heights. Our members appreciate the fact that we push the envelope and are not just another conventionally cautious and uncontroversial church.

Civilization has entered an unusually turbulent period and it is beginning to sink in that we are approaching the end of an era. The old cultural norms neither satisfy the individual, nor will they sustain the planet. Faith communities that are in touch with this reality, and that can help people shift their perspective in keeping with these changes, will not lack for involvement or support.

As a liberal religious institution, our mission and primary task in an unsettled age is not to offer, as Holloway puts it, "fixed and solid certainties that are likely to collapse under the pressure of events." Perhaps the best contribution we can make is to give today's anxious spiritual seekers the fresh insights, solid support, and honest encouragement that will allow them, in Holloway's words, "to change elegantly rather than awkwardly when the time is ripe."

DEVOTION

KEN BELDON

In Thoreau's age, as in our own, you were expected to choose sides. Refusing this cultural pressure to swear exclusive allegiance, Thoreau wrote in *A Week on the Concord and Merrimack Rivers*, "I know that some will have hard thoughts about me when they hear that their Christ is named beside my Buddha. Yet I am sure that I am willing they should love their Christ more than my Buddha, for love is the main thing."

For love is the main thing. Our capacity for devotion is more important religiously than the object of devotion.

Thoreau's words echo more notable ones from our Unitarian Universalist traditions, including Francis David's hope that "we need not think alike to love alike." David and Thoreau invite us to recognize and respect the natural diversity of our objects of love, while affirming the common human impulse of love that binds us. Devotion is a unifying force in life, beyond any dogma.

Starting in the summer of 2005, I would come to understand the meaning of devoted life in my ministry, as I took on a full commitment to a new life, whose course of growth I could not predict. I would help shape it, remaining focused on the "main thing" that Thoreau had identified.

I was about to become minister of a yet-to-be-named new UU congregation outside of Philadelphia. We had received generous financial support up front from sources throughout the denomination in the hope that we would grow in numbers. I was inspired by this investment in our faith.

I also knew that growing a congregation to grow a congregation is not a compelling mission. The formula for congregational vitality is more than "money + desire to see Unitarian Universalism expand its reach." Sunday morning attendance and numbers of members are manifestations of other kinds of less tangible, but absolutely essential, growth.

The best explanation for congregational health is clarity of mission and identity. I had learned this from the churches I had studied. Evangelical Christian Rick Warren calls it being a "purpose driven church." Tom Bandy, the consultant we worked with at WellSprings, calls it "congregational DNA."

But it's not only evangelical clergy and Christian consultants who stress the clarity of mission. UU minister Robert Latham, in his book *Moving On from Church Folly Lane*, teaches that vital congregations emphasize the experience of "diversity in unity," not the other way around. Mission is the common bond that gathers differences into a coherent and meaningful whole.

Long before WellSprings had a mission, I was reminded of Rabbi Abraham Joshua Heschel's words, that humanity "will not perish for want of information, but only for want of appreciation." I was convinced that the online Sunday *Times*, a comfy bathrobe, and a cup of coffee already had us beat as purveyors of information. The demographic data showed that many residents in the area we were going to serve increasingly chose this option.

But religious community promises something qualitatively different: the transformative capacity of human relationships that are grounded in the desire for religious awakening. I wanted to plant a congregation with that kind of identity. No amount of knowledge, study, or programming could guarantee this outcome. Only a leap of faith might make it a reality.

And I wasn't the only one making the leap. WellSprings began as a small group called the Planting Team, half of whom were established Unitarian Universalists and half mostly unchurched seekers, people on the periphery of the UU world or new to it. Starting in the fall of 2005, we worked together every week over nine months to create, then articulate, the identity of our congregation.

The small-group experience continues to be central to our congregational identity. As we began as a small group, so we continue to be a congregation of small groups. These "springboards" provide the relational and formational context for congregants to go deeper in exploration and spiritual maturity. Springboards meet once a week for ten consecutive weeks and turn over three times a year, ensuring that our small groups don't become closed, static cultures within the congregation. This fluid system gives people the chance to make more intensive but time-limited commitments. Regularly refreshed groups also break down barriers between established folks and newcomers.

One of our mantras very early on was this: As we began, so would we become. Beginnings set precedents. Questions about where we would worship, or what programs we'd offer, or how we were going to build the leadership structure of the congregation were important but secondary. We were committed to keeping first things first. Primary for us were the why and the who of launching a new congregation.

As a team of planters, we asked ourselves, Why is it so important to create a new religious community in the first place, and whom do we yearn to serve? We believed that the central reason for this congregation to come to life in the first place—the only reason it would be worthy of becoming a religious community that grew in numbers—was to offer a place where people could experience real personal spiritual growth and where the sacred experiences of awe and awakening and wisdom and justice and compassion and loving kindness would be our reasons for being. We wanted to serve people who hungered for these things as well.

Why? and who? are devotional questions that get at the heart of the true meaning of faith. Rather than understanding faith as a dogma or doctrine to be intellectually affirmed, James Fowler, author of *Stages of Faith*, writes that faith is "the center of experience [in which our] center becomes a participation in God or ultimate reality." Faith is a devotional act that requires commitment and vision but also humility and a radical receptivity to new ideas. For the Planting Team, that meant learning from unusual sources, even those that are sometimes hostile to religious progressives.

We found that we could learn from evangelical Christians without endorsing their theologies or social teachings. At WellSprings, our attitude has been that of the bank robber Willie Sutton. When asked why he robbed banks, he replied, "Because that's where the money is." We studied growing religious communities of all varieties so we could learn what we thought could help us. We did so because that was where the "money" was.

At a church planters' conference, I watched a fanciful video of a plane being flown while it was still being built. That's what planters do, the presenters said. Devotion to a vision precedes the full understanding of the form that vision will take. To get WellSprings off the ground, we needed faith in the creative powers of authentic religious growth and the cultivation of spiritual presence in relationship. The shape of our plane would continue to be created once we were in the air.

With the explicit trust and autonomy granted us by our denominational supporters—especially the extraordinary folks at Main Line Unitarian Church, who gifted us the time and money to develop and prepared the ground for us before WellSprings even had a name—we were able to begin the why and the who, reserving the programmatic and tactical questions for later.

In many ways, it wasn't a growth consultant but Diana Ross and the Supremes who were our wisest teachers early on—you can't hurry love. You can't force trust. Our work was urgent but not hasty. Church planters learn this lesson quickly. Devotion cannot be demanded; it must be offered freely.

So for the first three months, the Planting Team gathered each week. Together, we talked, shared personal stories, prayed and meditated, read ancient and modern wisdom, drew pictures, listened to music, studied some other congregations and traditions, and got to know each other through a program we called "Listening to Our Lives."

All the while we knew that, a year or more down the road, we would be launching a worshiping community. We never lost sight of that goal, but we knew that the only way we could eventually offer something meaningful beyond ourselves was to begin sharing meaningfully between ourselves. Like attracts like just as deep calls to deep.

Each week we centered on the animating questions that religious seekers have always asked and divided them into topics: Inspiration, the Sharing of Gifts, the Cultivation of Spiritual Practices and Disciplines, the Challenge of Suffering and the Lessons of Compassion, the Beauty of Grace, the Presence and Expectations of Beloved Community, the Experience of God and Ultimate Reality, the Acceptance of Our Mortality, and the Formation of Wholeness and Flourishing in This Life. These were the stories, ideas, and experiences around which we gathered for those three months.

At the end of that time, we didn't have anything like a mission or vision statement. What we had was more powerful: the experience of trusting one another and of having implicit permission to go deeper and challenge and encourage each other. As we began, so would we become.

We needed that trust to start articulating our DNA: our core values, beliefs, vision, and mission. We knew that we could offer the world only something we already possessed with integrity, an experience that we wanted to share in joy and with humility.

We knew we were on the right track when, a few months into our flight, several of the Planting Team members described our time together so far using images of wholeness, integration, and new beginnings—concepts that William James called "twice-born." Not the provenance of evangelical Christianity only, these universal experiences are about entering a life more abundant—calls of the soul that we felt compelled to answer. They oftentimes called us beyond the comfort of what we already knew so that we might grow into what we could become.

In that first single cell of WellSprings, we experienced what the great psychologist Abraham Maslow describes in his classic text, *Religions, Values, and Peak-Experiences.* Maslow, clearly sympathetic to the aims of liberal religion and Unitarianism (and Universalism) writes, "Any religion, liberal or orthodox, must not only be intellectually credible, and morally worthy of respect, but it must be emotionally satisfying as well. And I include here the transcendent emotions, as well."

Maslow was writing about those oceanic feelings of belonging, of peace that surpasses understanding, of a deep and abiding joy that is stronger and wiser than momentary pleasure. He was writing about the core religious experiences that transcend dogma, and he also challenged any religion that tried to reduce the holy to a single concept in order to either contain or critique it.

As we started to give shape to our DNA at WellSprings, we wanted to articulate a vision of Unitarian Universalism that implicitly asked questions such as, "How whole are we?" and "How whole are you?" and "How much are we flourishing together, and how do we equip each other to flourish in this life?"

We aimed to move beyond the extremes of individualism rampant in American culture. As our friendly critic Robert Bellah noted in 1998, at the UUA General Assembly in Rochester, New York, individualism can be the shadow side of our historically robust commitment to respect the conscience of the individual. He challenged us to remember that interdependence is a core aspect of our UU world view as well, and that our individual freedom finds its fulfillment in our connection with each other.

In our congregational DNA, we were mindful of the critique that UUs, sometimes justly, make against dogmatic Christianity: that in preaching the religion about Jesus, it forgets the religion of Jesus. Mindful of those posters that proclaim "Famous Unitarian Universalists" and display the blessed likenesses of Murray, Channing, Barton, Thoreau, Emerson, and Fuller, we checked ourselves. Are we going to build a religious community that merely conveys the facts of their lives? Or, incorporating these facts, will we also strive to build a community that encourages us to model their faith?

In our values and beliefs, in our vision and mission, we affirm that all true spirituality is incarnational. Wisdom is worn in the body and shared through the everyday quality of our lives. The content of our religious character is expressed through the shape of our care and compassion. Walt Whitman describes this incarnation in his amazing poem, "I Sing the Body Electric," from which we at WellSprings take our vision and our mission. That body electric, of both individuals and the whole congregation, strives for integration between body and heart and mind, and adds up to something more than its individual parts. Our mission calls us to be "A Community Charged Full with the Charge of the Soul."

Motivated by our mission, we started making decisions about the shape of our worship. We didn't choose proven techniques or cultural fads. Instead, we were inspired by a vision of how a charged-full congregation experiences itself in worship. We designed a worship service that called forth thought and feeling, celebration and sadness, reason and emotion, stillness and movement, raucous laughter and deep silence, and that, above all, invited the spirit to be present. We also believed that the charge was open to all ages, inviting not just adults but especially children. Our worship service is designed to help people experience greater wholeness and integration in their lives, to take down some of those barriers between the sacred and the profane that divide our lives and diminish our energies.

One Sunday after worship, a woman visiting with her nine-year-old son told me they'd definitely be returning. They would come back for several reasons, she said, but most particularly she was struck by her son's excitement over our energized music. He recognized a tune we were singing as something he had heard on the radio and exclaimed, "Mom, they're singing a *real* song!" At WellSprings, our contemporary worship helps people make connections between life inside the congregation and life beyond it.

Dr. Andrew Newberg, a radiologist and associate professor at the nearby University of Pennsylvania Medical School, studies "neurotheology." Through studies of the brain during spiritual practice, he has demonstrated that human beings are hardwired for spiritual experiences and growth. Through practice, we can cultivate compassion, insight, happiness, and loving kindness, though this is hardly news to any person from a contemplative tradition.

Because we encourage the integration of spiritual formation into everyday life, spiritual practice is an essential part of what membership and belonging mean at WellSprings. We felt called to make spiritual practice one of our core values because it resonates with our sense that religious wisdom is a naturally abundant resource. That insight belongs to no single tradition and requires no supernatural claim to back it up. Indeed, we can remain humble, even at times skeptical, of assigning ultimate attribution of these effects to any single source, but we don't have to deny the reality of the effect, and the essential, formative nature of spiritual practice in religious growth.

We believe that spiritual practice offers a common ground of experience for people from both theistic and nontheistic aspects of our living tradition. By emphasizing practice alongside conceptual classification of religious life, our DNA encourages us to find common ground in the experiential dimensions of our spirituality. That means that we do not just think daily about our spiritual lives. Through contemplation, prayer, meditation, sacred reading, reflection, and gathering with others, we equip ourselves and each other for religious growth.

Although worship is the central, shared expression of our life together, we recognize that Sunday morning is just one hour, and if Sunday morning is the only hour that we are getting religion, then WellSprings is failing in its mission. We believe the purpose of Sunday morning is to sustain, equip, and celebrate the kind of religion that comes about through daily practice. Our Sunday service is an invitation to a life of greater devotion, to a greater awareness and understanding of all that is our life.

Our DNA also keeps us open to the insights of someone like Sam Harris, the nontheist writer and ardent opponent of organized religion. After offering some surprising praise for certain contemplative practices at the American Atheist Alliance meeting in 2007, Harris concluded, "These contemplative experiences have a lot to say about the plasticity of the human mind and about the possibilities of human happiness."

In WellSprings DNA, we aspire to realize what Harris articulated in his message. We believe in a cultivated expansiveness that brings us to that deeper place of knowing greater possibilities of human happiness—the kind of happiness found not in things or in possessions, but in living fully, loving generously, and being who we are called to be. We're talking about practicing the arts of awakening, of flourishing as human beings. We believe that is where the really interesting, fruitful conversation and practice is in today's religious life.

The one thing we can say about that kind of conversation is that thinking alone will not get us there. Maslow is absolutely right: Some things must first be experienced, and we must give ourselves over to them in devotion. Only later can they be understood, filtered through our rational minds upon reflection.

Emerson, in his 1838 Divinity School Address, said beautifully and succinctly, "Faith makes us, and not we it." He balanced his claim upon self-reliance with a bow in the direction of grace. This other, necessary side of Emerson's thought is a devotional complement to the active and rational strain in our living religious tradition. Devotion calls us to surrender some of our illusions of control.

Our congregational commitment to devotion doesn't mean that we focus on ourselves alone. Inwardness can be a form of narcissism, and we cannot wait for the perfect day when we are mature enough to move beyond ourselves as a new congregation—that day will not arrive. In WellSprings' two and a half years as a worshiping community, we've given away over $25,000 to local antihunger initiatives and providers of health care for the uninsured. We've funded and participated in the building of a Habitat House and sent volunteers the last two summers to cultivate a local nonprofit organic farm that models sustainable practices and wise use of the land.

These acts lead us into deeper relationships with people in our area and will perhaps birth more wide-ranging commitments in time to come. At WellSprings, we proclaim a Unitarian Universalism that is more than just about "deeds, not creeds." Our calling is to live from the inside out, where what we do is reflective of who we truly are as members of a spiritual community.

The other, outward signs of our growth are present and positive. In just over two years since we launched our worship services, our average Sunday attendance has reached over 150 people, peaking near 200. In the fall of 2009, we added a second worship service, so our growth will be sustainable, and we will have room for all who seek our spiritual community. All the while as we grow, we remind ourselves of what makes that growth possible in the first place.

Launching a new religious community has been a kind of ongoing experiment in devotion. As with all new life, the desire to simply be often outstrips the practical knowledge that is required to thrive. A friend of mine who planted a new spiritual community fondly quotes the title of a book: *The Answer to How Is Yes*. As we meet new and emerging life at WellSprings, we return again and again to the fundamental attitude of trust that called us to create something new in the first place.

Willingness is the first step in making a way. We trust our devotion to call us back to the disciplined practice of being in community, of learning what needs to be learned so that our dreams can come alive. As we began, so will we become.

Mission

THOM BELOTE

Many Unitarian Universalists first heard about Carlton Pearson when National Public Radio's *This American Life* dedicated a full hour to telling his life story. In its simplest form, the story goes that Pearson was a charismatic Pentecostal preacher who became a disciple of Oral Roberts, won a Grammy for gospel music, and founded Higher Dimensions, a successful megachurch in Tulsa, Oklahoma. The story continues that Pearson had a theological epiphany, adopted a universalist theology of salvation, and consequently was shunned by the evangelical community for his heresy and deserted by his followers because he strayed from the path of orthodoxy. As I write this, the remnant of his congregation is going through the process of combining with All Souls Unitarian Church in Tulsa.

I want to focus on one miniscule part of Pearson's fascinating story. After he had openly embraced universalism but before the doors of Higher Dimensions closed, a friend of mine frequently attended this congregation. During a phone conversation five years ago, my friend happened to mention the mission statement of Higher Dimensions: To exalt the savior, equip the saints, and evangelize the world.

As I wrote the last paragraph, I did not have to pause and try to pull that mission statement from the recesses of my memory. I did not have to go looking through notes and writings to see if I could find it. I did not have to search the Internet. It was available to me by instant recall. I can remember the mission statement of a church I've never attended, led by a minister I've never heard, a mission statement that was quoted to me once during a phone conversation five years ago.

Let me make this plain: I can instantly tell you the mission statement of a church I've never visited, but I bet that you, dear reader, cannot tell me the mission statement of your Unitarian Universalist congregation. I want to issue you a challenge. Put this book down. Pick up a pen and a scrap of paper. Write down what you think the mission statement of your church is. Then go compare what you've written to the actual mission statement as it appears (if it appears) on your church website, or as it might be written in your congregation's latest newsletter. If you can't find it there, call your church office or a board member and ask them to tell you the mission statement of your congregation. The person you call may put you on hold and go digging through file folders.

On the surface, the issue of mission statements may seem very small. Yet, they reflect something quite important: the need for members of a congregation to be aligned in a common purpose, to be articulate about why they exist and what they are in the world to do, and to achieve clarity in this understanding. A guiding mission statement can align the programs of a church and keep them from being scattershot, at best, and counterproductive, at worst.

In their book, *When Moses Meets Aaron*, Gil Rendle and Susan Beaumont write, "Despite their importance, mission statements are too general and attempt to speak for too long of a time period, which prevents them from providing clear and immediate direction for ministry." Spending a little time perusing the websites of Unitarian Universalist congregations reveals (in the cases where a mission statement can actually be found) that many of our congregations have mission statements that "speak for too long" and fail to provide "clear and immediate direction for ministry." Often their content is predictable, and they resemble something like the following:

> We aspire to be a welcoming, intergenerational community that respects individual differences and beliefs. Together, we share the joys and milestones of life as we foster intellectual

inquiry and spiritual understanding. In the larger community we promote social action and environmental responsibility.

There doesn't seem to be anything wrong with this mission statement. But dig a little deeper and the problems begin to surface. This paragraph is impossible to remember. At three sentences, it is shorter than many, but by the time you finish reading, you forget how it begins. A mission statement needs to be memorable. At its best, it is a declaration that you will remember five years after hearing it once.

If your minister or your key lay leaders can't recite the mission statement from memory, then you don't actually have a mission statement. If the majority of members in your congregation can't recite the mission statement, then you still don't actually have one. When crafting a mission statement, the goal should be that if someone visits your church once, she should be able to say what it is when asked on the way out to the parking lot.

One reason the sample mission statement is impossible to memorize is that it is full of implied contradictions. Take a look at that middle sentence again. "Joys and milestones." "Intellectual inquiry and spiritual understanding." Lists like these, even when they are short, seem inclusive. But inclusive of whom? The statement implies that the members of the congregation do not share a common purpose —but that this is just fine. It implies that there is a division between those who seek spiritual understanding and those who come for intellectual inquiry. And consider the third sentence—mentioning environmental responsibility separately from social action implies some struggle between those for whom environmental responsibility is of primary importance and those who see it as an aspect of the larger work of social justice.

In this mission statement, the lists follow bland and passionless verbs: *aspire, be, respect, share, foster,* and *promote.* Two of the verbs—*aspire* and *respect*—are actionless. They are thinking verbs that require no expenditure of energy. Two more of the verbs—*share* and *promote*—are talking words. In order to share or to promote, all people really have to do is open their mouths. The most active verb is to foster, but in this mission statement what is being fostered is intellectual stimulation and spiritual understanding—in other words, more talking. And then there is the verb to be. Hamlet may have used it to ponder the nature of existence, but any decent writing instructor will tell you to avoid it as much as possible. *To be* means "to exist," and while existing is certainly better than not existing, a church's mission should aim for something greater.

A close reading reveals still one more feature that is unfortunately all too common in Unitarian Universalist mission statements: the opt-out clause. In this example, it is found at the end of the first sentence, in the phrase "respects individual differences and beliefs." This line is far from harmless. By juxtaposing the idea of a "welcoming, intergenerational community" with respect for difference, the mission statement essentially says, "if you want to."

Some may refer to an opt-out clause as a "conscience clause" and claim that they are affirming the free conscience of their members. No community can claim 100 percent agreement on all matters. Even Jesus had a tough time getting all the disciples on the same page. But a mission statement should say, "Here is why we exist. Here is what we are in the world to do." It should not say, "Here is why we exist but you should feel free to disagree."

The problem with many Unitarian Universalist mission statements is not that they are virtually impossible to memorize. And the problem is not that these statements are full of implied contradictions, weak verbs, and clauses that conspire to undermine a sense of common purpose. The problem is that the mission statements developed by congregations too often reflect the actual congregations for which they are written. They fail to prioritize and to discern which actions and values are most important. They wrongly equate being directive, or missional, with being exclusionary.

In 2003, I became the minister of the Shawnee Mission Unitarian Universalist Church in Overland Park, Kansas. Shawnee Mission had been stuck on a plateau of between 175 and 200 adult members for much of the previous decade. Even a building addition that added much-needed worship space and six new religious education classrooms did not significantly impact the size of the congregation. Bolstered by a test-drive of the UUA advertising campaign in the Kansas City metro area in the six months prior to my arrival, Shawnee Mission experienced rapid growth. As we raced toward 300 adult members, we added staff, added a second worship service, and otherwise negotiated our identity as a solidly program-sized church. We also formed a long-range planning committee, whose first task was to lead the congregation through a mission and vision process.

As this group diligently worked toward the creation of a mission statement, I received a query from a member of the congregation, who asked, "Why are we going through this process again?" We did have a mission statement, I was assured, though the details were a bit fuzzy. What did it say? Who had created it? When was it created? What happened to it? No answers came.

During a slow day at the office, I decided to launch *CSI: Shawnee Mission* and embarked on a thorough forensic investigation. I called church leaders, looking for clues or possible leads. After hours of searching, I discovered that the board had developed a mission statement nearly five years before I arrived. It read:

> Our church values and promotes the search for spirituality, tolerance, knowledge, and love. We seek truth, compassion, and acceptance by nurturing and respecting the thoughts of all individuals. Our members and friends promote the building of community through inclusion and the honoring of all voices.

Without belaboring the point, it is telling that the mission statement of the church was not included in any of the documents the congregation put forth when they were searching for a new minister. Once again—if the minister does not know that the congregation has a mission statement, much less what it actually says, the congregation does not have a mission statement.

The first objective of the long-range planning team at Shawnee Mission was to formulate mission and vision statements. This team communicated with the membership through surveys, membership meetings, and a visioning session as part of the worship services. Then they began shaping all the opinions and input into mission and vision statements.

When I met with these lay leaders, I shared with them the example of the mission statement from Higher Dimensions Church. In nine words and three alliterative phrases, Higher Dimensions had formed a nearly perfect mission statement. The one we came up with at Shawnee Mission turned out to be almost as good. It read:

INVITE everyone into caring community

INSPIRE the search for spiritual growth

INVOLVE each person in working for a peaceful, fair, and free world

The statement has a lot going for it. It is fairly easy to remember. Even if you have a hard time memorizing the whole thing, it is easy to recite the three alliterative verbs. The mission statement is not perfect—if I had my way, I would eliminate "the search for" from the second clause, and replace "a peaceful, fair, and free world" with words that are even more succinct. But we avoided writing a bland paragraph that is eminently forgettable. The three clauses are catchy.

And they caught on. Not only do I remember the words, but staff, lay leaders, and many members do as well. And our mission statement does more than exist. It is actually used. Now when we talk about how we are doing as a church, we use the words *invite, inspire,* and *involve.* "How are we doing at being inviting?" "Are you feeling inspired?" "Where are you involved?" The language is contagious.

A few observations can be made about our mission statement. First, I make no claims about causality. Shawnee Mission was already growing before we formulated our statement, and it continued to grow afterward. This doesn't mean the mission statement wasn't an important aspect of our growth. It also doesn't mean that all you need to do is come up with a catchy, pithy mission statement to create growth. Rather, it was our willingness to attempt to be precise and concise about the mission of Shawnee Mission that promoted growth.

Second, having a useful mission statement requires discipline. After publishing and promoting the mission statement to the church, we actually used it. We framed activities, programs, and initiatives in terms of fulfilling this mission. When we expanded a staff position or made a new hire, we asked how doing so would help us to be more inviting, inspiring, or involving. Our decision making became more disciplined. We aligned ourselves in common purpose, growing articulate about and achieving clarity as to why we exist and what we are in the world to do.

Third, if you chafe at the idea of a mission statement and consider it too restrictive or too limiting, remember that a mission statement is not the end of a conversation but the beginning of one. Unitarian Universalists understand that scripture is meant to be interpreted and not meant to be taken literally. We should approach mission statements the same way. Leaders and staff at Shawnee Mission engaged in rich discussions and deep deliberations about what it really meant to invite, inspire, and involve. But these discussions were focused. They were centered. We shared ideas about how to fulfill this mission and, although these ideas varied profoundly, we were aligned in trying to achieve our goals.

Having a pithy and memorable mission statement is related to congregational growth in a significant, though indirect manner. As far as I know, not a single soul has ever joined a religious community because of its alluring mission statement. And probably only the most contentious and inflexible of souls would leave a religious community because of the way it articulated its mission. It is not the mission statement itself, but rather how it is lived, that is of consequence.

If a religious community is like a large boat traveling across the sea, its mission is like a map of where it wants to go on the journey. Without a mission, the boat is merely adrift, susceptible to the whims of wind and surf, or it is commandeered by whoever is the most opinionated and determined to seize control of its steering wheel. Having a clear mission helps us to know that we are en route toward our goals.

People come to a church for all sorts of reasons. As I talk to those coming into our church, I realize that the old joke that the definition of a Unitarian Universalist is an atheist with children is now less true than it once was. There are certainly those who "came for their children, but stayed for themselves." But the reasons are expanding. Many come as spiritual seekers looking for a spiritual practice that is not isolating. Others come seeking to reshape their lives and to make a difference in the world. Many come because they are facing something that they do not want to face alone. It is not only negative things—disease, grieving, unemployment—that bring them to us; sometimes even something positive, like partnership or parenting, causes them to seek community. More and more, we encounter those who are deeply restless and feel that something is missing in their lives, and who are looking to become more complete. A mission statement helps to let them know where the boat is headed.

Let me return to a question I asked earlier: Can your minister, your staff, your lay leaders, the members of your congregation, and even a person who glances at your website or visits your congregation once or twice tell you what the mission statement is? If not, you do not really have a mission statement. You have something else: a paragraph. A mission statement that is well constructed, catchy, and powerful brings the work of the congregation into focus, joining clarity of purpose with direction.

Because you are reading this book, you are probably interested in ways to promote growth in your congregation. The bad news is that there is no magic formula, no silver bullet, no magic bean. If there were, this book would be a whole lot shorter. The subjects of all of these essays are important in promoting growth, but none of them is the answer in and of itself.

But when creating your mission statement, dare to be clear. Dare to be focused. Dare to use active verbs that describe the changes that happen to individuals and to society as a result of your congregation's actions. Don't worry if a few members disagree. It is better to have a mission statement of substance for them to push against than to have one so lacking in substance that it supports no one. Keep your mission before you. Try your best to live it as you continue your journey.

WORSHIP

VICTORIA SAFFORD

On early Sunday mornings, when the sanctuary is still dark, I am alone, straightening the chairs, checking the thermostat, setting the hymn books evenly among the pews, and wondering, although I hold the order of service firmly in my hands, what may ensue in that room over the next hours. More frequently than I would like, a passage from Annie Dillard's *Teaching a Stone to Talk* comes to mind:

> Week after week I climbed the long steps to that little church, entered, and took a seat with some few of my neighbors. Week after week I was moved by the pitiableness of the bare, linoleum-floored sacristy, which no flowers could cheer or soften, by the terrible singing I so loved, by the fatigued Bible readings, the lagging emptiness and dilution of the liturgy, the horrifying vacuity of the sermon, and by the fog of dreary senselessness pervading the whole, which existed alongside and probably caused, the wonder of the fact that we came; we showed up; week after week, we went through with it.

In a couple of hours, our people will start to arrive. What will they find in this space, set apart from other spaces, within the clearing of an hour set aside from all their other busy hours? "Lagging emptiness" and "horrifying vacuity" are ever-present possibilities, but I'm longing for reverence and relevance, for worship that touches the soul. In a couple of hours, we will speak Rebecca Edmiston-Lange's Call to Worship as we do every Sunday: "Come in. Come into this place which you make holy by your presence . . ." What can that mean? What is this thing we are trying to do?

On Sunday morning, we worship by engaging in spiritual practice. For some, this time is the only spiritual practice in their week or in their lives. We come separately, and join together, to practice our religion. This is a serious business—a joyful, artful, imperfect, serious business.

Chinese philosopher Lao Tse said that if we would know the One Thing (the great truth, the great mystery, the Holy), we must know it through "the ten thousand things." That is, the sacred or god or whatever It is can be known only through the ordinary, through the ten thousand ways that the world, nature, and art, other people, tables, chairs, and all earthbound things show themselves to us. Our relationships with each other and with the known world reflect the relationship we would have with the Infinite, the Eternal, the One. If only It weren't so infinite and eternal, we could grasp It and know It face-to-face. As it is, with our little hands, we can grasp only each other; with our little limited eyes, we can see (and love and praise) only this world, these ten thousand things. Only through our daily practices, habits, and rituals, and our ways of ordering the day or arranging our communities—which seem intuitive and automatic but are really quite deliberate—can we glimpse something of the One Thing, of the sacred.

The opening of eyes and heart, the clearing of mind to prepare for worship must be done with purpose. That's what spiritual practice is, whether you're walking the dog, praying your prayers, chanting a chant, or coming to church. It's also about placement. For those who worship in the woods or near water, it's about looking at herons and knowing that, just as surely as their work in this world is to lift from pond to sky in one silent symphony of motion, our work in this world is to notice. More than that, our spiritual work is to place ourselves, deliberately, punctually, and regularly, in the company of whatever sacred presence or holy absence—whether bird or music or blank journal page or scripture or gathered congregation—will call us back to who and what we are.

Notice. Look. Wonder. Give thanks. Mourn. Repent. *Repeat.*

It's the repetition of spiritual practice that matters, over and over, and the showing up, in place, on time. A church may be one good place for this practice, and Sunday morning one good time.

But the service is not the thing itself. The sermon, the music, the silences, the speaking of names in the meditation, the movement of the morning light across the walls of a beloved sanctuary (the way that it has moved for years and years) and over the faces of a beloved community: None of these is the thing itself, but any of them may open the spirit to it. Thus, we prepare the service with care. The sermon is written—no matter who writes it, member or minister, resident or guest—the hymns chosen and rehearsed, the music prepared, the readings and readers selected, the room made lovely, all with great care and reverence. If I am a stickler for preparation, it's because on Sundays I feel as if we're readying the house for long-awaited guests or for family returning home after many days away. And so it is. To prepare well is a deliberate act of hospitality, welcoming anyone who may show up, and also the holy, which may, by grace, show up.

Unlike almost every other thing we do with purpose, worship makes nothing, accomplishes nothing, sells nothing, yields nothing. It is its own end. In our liberal communion, worship has no direct object; the verb is intransitive. We don't worship any single thing but draw instead upon the meaning of the Old English weorthscipe: "to consider that which is of worth, to hold that which is worthy." We remember what has worth, once a week, for a little while, together. To honor what is worthy of honor, to notice what is worthy of notice, to grieve the losses and the sorrows that are worthy of our tears, to tell stories about and sing about, to celebrate, to draw closer to, to be more mindful of what matters; to name, in the clearest possible language, with the best possible music, through the deepest possible silence, a few significant things.

Of the 168 hours in a week, we set one aside precisely for this work that is not exactly work, this activity that isn't very active (neither is it passive) and that yields no product—except sometimes a kind of deepening. A shifting of perspective. An interior transformation. A revelation. Sometimes, by luck or grace, we may glimpse something invisible: a sense of reassurance, acceptance, comfort, or peace—whether peace of mind or peacefulness of spirit—sufficient for the hours and days ahead. We may feel gratitude, forgiveness, resolution. We may feel an unwelcome and uneasy challenge to calcified conviction, an unexpected stirring to more concerted courage, or a call for actionable outrage, when outrage is what's needed in the world beyond the self. These feelings are immeasurable, intangible, and are not felt by everyone at once. Worship for us is communal and yet essentially private. Who knows how far anyone may travel between the Prelude and the Closing Words?

In *The Sabbath*, Abraham Joshua Heschel, the great Jewish theologian, describes the Sabbath as a "great cathedral" in "the architecture of time." He marks the old correspondence, in Latin, between *templar* (temple) and *tempus* (time). The Sabbath is a temple, a cathedral, made of time:

> Six days a week, we live under the tyranny of things in space; on the Sabbath we try to become attuned to holiness in time. It is a day on which we are called upon to share in what is eternal in time, to turn from the results of creation to the mystery of creation; from the world of creation to the creation of the world.

By this he meant not only the origins of the world, but its continuous renovation, which is ours to imagine, to hope for, fight for, and bring about. In its oldest form, *liturgy* means "the people's work." That's what worship is and what worship leads to—ritual, art, prayer, conversation and argument, the establishment of covenants and right relations with each other, ethics, stories and play, and hard work—all the ways by which we re-create the world. Again, worship reminds us, in the words of our Call to Worship, of "who we are, and who we're called to be."

It is Friday morning, and I am in the home of my friends Stephan and Naomi, celebrating the birth of their first child. The house is a cozy, festive chaos, filled with food and neighbors and children and relatives crowded in from far away, all suddenly brought to hushed silence as a white-clad officiant begins his chanted prayers, and the tiny baby is carried in on a great embroidered pillow. When I arrived, the officiant was just an ordinary person eating chips and salsa, chortling about the Red Sox and the traffic coming into town. Now, in his robes, he is transformed. The baby is asleep, clearly unaware that on this eighth day of his life, he will be brought into the covenant of his people with God through the ritual of circumcision.

The mohel begins to chant, and suddenly we have stepped through a door in time. There is a sense that all of this has taken place before, especially in the responses of the older relatives: the way they compose themselves for singing, the way they rhythmically answer the prayers ("Amen and amen"), the way they do not flinch when the tiny knife is raised. This has all happened before, but it is also new, unprecedented; it is not a mechanical rite. For the parents, self-declared secular, nonpracticing Jews, it's clear that everything is strange and wonderful, a little fearsome, even though they've both seen circumcisions many times before. It is as if their boy is the first to be so honored since Isaac was circumcised by Abraham, and they are themselves Abraham and Sarah, laughing for joy and pale with apprehension. "Give the mother some wine before I start," says the mohel, "and the boy too." I thought he meant Stephan, but he meant the baby, who is given drops from a grandmother's finger. Naomi, who doesn't drink, gulps a full glass and sits down.

The ritual is older than memory and renews us all. When the prayers are spoken—May you speak with righteous words and act with righteous deeds—we feel suddenly that this might be possible, that we might even lend a hand toward bringing it about. We are swept, right there, into the waves of human history, into space and time transformed. Then it is over, and Micah with his beautiful new name is bandaged up and rocked to sleep by his grandmothers, and we all shout, "Mazel tov!" and turn to the fabulous food.

Ritual matters. On Sundays in our churches and at other times, in other places, ritual grounds and centers the community, confirms its identity and purpose, and sometimes transforms the lives of those within it.

In the same week as Micah's circumcision, I stood in a cemetery with a different family, conducting a different ritual for a different baby, who died at birth. The extended family gathered there was Roman Catholic, but the parents themselves were not anymore, and they knew in their hearts that they could not have a funeral mass for their child. Present in the circle, swaddled in her mother's arms, was another baby, the twin sister of the one who had died.

In the cemetery, in the pouring rain, under the little plastic canopy that the funeral home provides, we made a circle. I took two red roses and for each of the two infants spoke the words of dedication:

> The water in this chalice is a sign of the sources from which all life springs. It reminds us that we are forever connected to the earth and the elements, and that we are connected to each other. Of water and earth and star-stuff are we made and this water reminds us: Today we embrace you within our community, but we know you are already held within the embrace of the great community of beings—you are part of the wholeness and the holiness of the very world.

Twice I asked, "By what name is this child known?" and twice I said, "We dedicate you in the love of your parents, in the caring of your family, and in the larger love that transcends all our understanding." The people repeated the same words of gratitude and wonder, the brave and joyful words about the remaking of the world that we say when babies are dedicated in our church on Sunday mornings. Then we turned and placed another rose, a white one, on the little coffin and spoke different words, invoking the same mystery but choked with sorrow and an impossible farewell. At the end, the mother smiled at her family and told them through her tears how grateful she was that they were there, that they would stand with her, outside of their church, making holy ground for her and her husband and their child to stand on. She told them that on this date every year, despair and joy would intersect, and that, because they had cast this circle, she would be able to hold both her daughters always, one in memory, and one right there, and there'd be no gladness without sorrow, and no grief without unending gratitude.

How did this family know what they needed to do? In *Religious Worlds*, William Paden, a scholar of religions, writes:

> Ritual is the deliberate structuring of action and time to give focus, expression and sacredness to what would otherwise be diffuse, unexpressed, or profane. Ritual is a sacred action and time deliberately created. Like any behavior, ritual can degenerate into a mechanical act. But in its essential nature, it is an act of concentrated display with regard to some particular purpose.
>
> Ritual constructs its own space. It is time that can be "entered" by participants. It is time that has an inside. Such times are like sanctuaries, with an interiority of their own . . . and within that area everything incongruous has been kept away. . . . Like a picture whose borders accentuate the image while simultaneously marking off the impertinences and interferences of everything outside the border, such a frame at once enhances its own contents and sets off everything extraneous. In this sense, ritual time is analogous to ritual space.
>
> Once within the potency of the ritual circle, time assumes a charged quality. Within the hothouse of its frame, the content of that time becomes real, alive, effective. With the closing off of the outside world, the inner world of the ritual becomes resonant with its own life, its own momentousness, and its own sense of the holy and eternal.

On that Friday morning in my friends' most ordinary living room, the chairs were pushed back, the prayers were chanted, an extraordinary space was established, and we were swept into the very covenant of Abraham. That same week, on Tuesday, I got up from the desk, the computer, the phone, and went out into the ordinary rain to the graveyard. People gathered there and—out of nothing—made a temple, a circle so strong it could hold the mysteries of birth and death, which like the wind came howling in. That which transcends our understanding comes in and down and all around, and we are in it, and it is in each of us, on an otherwise ordinary day. This extraordinary circumstance may be brought about by the simplest ritual on any ordinary Sunday in our congregations.

Liturgy means "the people's work," and worship is a most physical labor. It is done deliberately. Even if the ritual is simply sitting there in meditation, one must first get into the room, prepare the room, sit down in the room. Lighting candles means driving to Target or who knows what unholy place to get the candles and the matches. Holding hands in silence with your family before dinner (such a simple act of grace) means deciding in advance whether you mind that someone's hands are almost always sticky, washed or not, or whether someone's idea of silence includes humming pretty loudly the song he learned in preschool that day.

Ritual is contrived, human-made, active; it does not just happen. Novelist Peter Devries once told *The Observer*, "I write when I'm inspired, and I see to it that I'm inspired at nine o'clock every morning." At church, we see to it that we're ready to be inspired at nine and eleven every Sunday, rain or shine.

Ritual is a chore, and there is nothing mysterious or strange or magical in preparing for it. You arrange the furniture. You cook the meal. You buy the wine on sale at the discount liquor store and carry it home in a paper bag, before decanting it into your grandmother's sacred silver goblets. You arrange to meet at the cemetery, the sanctuary, the living room, and you make the reservations and order the flowers and the canopy. Someone remembers to fill the bowl with water from the faucet in the bathroom; someone buys long matches for the chalice so the children are less likely to be singed. I ran into someone from church at the supermarket late one Saturday night, who was amazed that I was buying roses for a dedication the next day. "You buy them *here?*" she said. "At *Stop and Shop?*" I think she'd imagined some sacred arbor out behind the Social Hall.

Sacred rituals require getting everything together by whatever means you can—except everything that you forget—then taking a breath and sliding into place, sometimes late but not too late. And if it all sounds sort of grubby and mundane, that's because it is grubby and mundane. Even archbishops and high priests have someone ironing their vestments and washing the communion cup each week with detergent that won't dim the shine or leave unsightly spots. Liturgy is the people's work, the holy work of worship.

Even if you have done this thing, whatever it is, every day of your life, or even if your people have done it for generations, you wait and see what will occur. No matter what it is—graduation, ordination, confirmation, the solstice celebration or the Easter parade, holding hands at supper time or bringing out that gravy boat, that recipe, that memory, each year at Thanksgiving—you prepare as best you can and then wait to see what happens: what change, what transformation.

Ritual is art and sacrament, and we can't know what beauty, what hope and faith and love, what fear or sorrow, what new, expanded understanding it will manifest. We stand available. We are alert and awake, mindful that we are alive and fairly fragile, aware that there are some few things we can do together, on purpose, and many more things out of our control. The saving grace in Sunday morning is that it comes round again and again and again.

In our congregation on a typical Sunday, there are many voices in the room, many hands behind the scenes, and many opportunities to collaborate. Volunteers serve as greeters, readers, welcomers, chalice lighters, and musicians, invited by the Worship Committee, the minister, or the director of music to understand and undertake these roles. The committee is a dedicated community within the congregation, charged with consolidating their own wild and random opinions, styles, preferences, theologies, and longings, as well as everything they hear from everybody else, into careful guardianship of Sunday morning services. They hold in their hands the wheel of the year; the liturgical cycle of celebrations and observances; the congregation's traditions, history, and quirks. Like the Hospitality Committee perking coffee in the Social Hall, their charge is to nourish the people. Like the Religious Education team, they are concerned with what it means to grow a soul. Like the Art Committee, they traffic in beauty, and with the Social Action Committee, they ask, constantly, what it means to bear witness.

Into the circle so carefully cast, they invite the entire community: children, adults, youth, elders, long-time members and first-time visitors, the living and the dead. Into the pulpit they invite those who speak with skill and confidence and also those who don't. Into the choir they invite those who love to sing well and those who simply love to sing. Worship levels the playing field, inviting all to share the sacred ground. The members of the Worship Committee serve as referees and goalies; together with the minister, they write the rules of engagement. Ferociously, they guard the elegance of the hour, its specific form and predictable order, so that wild content can race around inside it: radical thoughts, dangerous, unorthodox ideas, searing exhortations, the slightly off-beat poem, the slightly off-key soloist, the screaming dedicated baby, the sermon's many, many imperfections.

I asked members of our committee what they think our Sunday worship is for. One person wrote, "We come to center ourselves, individually and together, and to then explore and search and question and offer and receive and reflect and relax and recharge and reveal to ourselves and maybe to each other, something of value, of worth, that will maybe guide us during the coming days or reveal to us the meaning of the days we have just journeyed through."

A long-time member said, "We come to join with others in an act of common prayer, and by doing so, hope to move beyond our narrow prejudices and personal concerns to embrace a larger vision of life."

Another person said, "Worship is a time to be open, a time to let in what one is now ready to hear, or what one now has found the strength to feel, something that maybe one was not ready to take in or to work with before, but now the time has arrived for that particular moment of growth."

Someone else wrote, "To me, worship is an active, participatory experience, as opposed to the presentation of a 'program.' My participation may appear to be very still and inward, or perhaps I may be an active catalyst, but in either case, or in any case, I am not a bystander." These are people who know the power of symbols and words. They also know and honor the diversity of needs and expectations in the congregation, the spoken and unspoken longings. They know that the sanctuary is not the only room of the house in which worship occurs—that it also happens in the Social Hall over coffee and in the parking lot, the classrooms, and quiet corners where grief is shared or fear confessed. It happens out on Highway 61, when every Monday our members stand with signs, resisting the current war. The committee simply seeks to sanctify one specific place, one particular hour. In guarding the gate, they open wide the door. They hold the fort, and the people let down their defenses.

About the third week after I became the minister of my first congregation, a venerable member stopped me in the parlor. She took my shaky hand in her gloved one and said, "I'm so glad you've come to us, dear. You have a most ... unusual ... approach. It's a real change for us; we used to have *intelligent* sermons week after week after week." After almost twenty years, I'm beginning to think I might try to take this as a compliment. Unitarian Universalist ministers are trained to understand that intellectual rigor, steel-trap reasoning, and the revelations of science matter very much in the way we do religion (in fundamentalist times, they matter more than ever). But they are not all that matter. Other dimensions of our humanity, other dimensions of mystery are of shining worth.

From Rumi, writing in the twelfth century, comes this ancient wisdom:,

If God said,
"Rumi, pay homage to everything
that has helped you

enter my

arms,"

there would not be one experience of my life,

not one thought, not one feeling, nor any act,

I would not bow to.

In our Unitarian Universalist tradition, we are privileged and burdened by the responsibility to pay homage to everything that makes us human. Our services are not and should not be all things to all people. They should not be random smorgasbords of interfaith fast food but should draw from many sources, many deep pools of thought, experience, and wisdom.

Not long ago, a child from that first congregation tracked me down on Facebook to ask an urgent question. I say "child" because that's what he was when I saw him last, a kid in the youth group in the church I served ten years ago. I thought I'd left him there, forever young in gauzy memory, but here he was writing from Andover Newton Theological School, where, at age thirty, he is in his first year of seminary. He asked me how to write sermons. This is part of what I sent to him:

> I say, first: **Read.** Broadly, widely, deeply, indiscriminately, lavishly. Read history, fiction, nonfiction, but poetry in particular, and also memoirs and autobiographies. Here you will find the most clear, honest, lyrical testimony about the human condition. Read, but also engage all the arts— music (Do you still play the flute?), dance, drama, painting, architecture—in forms that attract you and forms you find jarring. Again, these are all expressions of the human soul, in thousands of variations. Read aloud, as often as you can.
>
> Second: **Find your own voice.** This sounds so trite and so vague, but it is the foundation of good writing, and requisite to preaching with integrity, courage, and grace. Early in my ministry, I began a strange practice that I still keep: I write my sermons (and most other things, including this e-mail) out loud. In Northampton, I wrote mostly standing in the pulpit,

often late at night, speaking to a congregation I could see in my mind, individuals I was coming to love. I stood with a pen and yellow pad, speaking from the heart to them—and then scurried to the computer in my office, because my penmanship is so poor that I'd often lose entire paragraphs, and hours of work, if I didn't transcribe the lines quickly enough. Back and forth, from pulpit to keyboard, writing out loud to real people, some of whom called out to me in my imagination: "Very nice—but who cares? How does this relate to me?" or "You're speaking to my head, but not to my spirit" or "You're speaking to my soul, but ignoring my intelligence." "What exactly is your point?" And so on. The members of the conjured congregation were rigorous, patient critics and excellent teachers. I can conjure them still.

This strange process imposes several requirements:

I hold before me the lives, losses, loves of real people—not only my own little concerns, passions, questions.

Writing "out loud" forces the text on the page to conform to the cadence and tone of my speaking voice. It is authentic and also "preachable."

Writing it down, of course, forces art upon the spoken word: I want sentences and images that are lyrical, elegant, and beautiful (if possible), because I love language and mean to treat it with respect.

The writing process echoes and must be preceded by a process of prayer. The first conversation I must engage, whether out loud or silently, is an interior conversation with my own soul, and between that soul and that which transcends it. It is a conversation with God. This is not language I choose lightly nor often, but here it applies. I must write and preach what I know most deeply, and what I wonder, fear, love, trust. It is for this reason that

I find the writing process much more fearsome than the preaching process. By the time I face the congregation, I have wrestled with other, more terrible angels. This doesn't mean I'm confident, but at least I know I've already tried to travel whatever road I mean to take the people on that morning. This is also why my sermons tend to be full of unanswered, and unanswerable, questions more than proclamations. By Sunday morning, I have a pretty good sense of how little I know, and deep compassion for the unknowing we all share.

There were some funny moments in the Great Hall, as you can imagine. I'd be there in the dark, late at night, with just the little pulpit lamp to see by. I remember Sally coming in once to place some flowers, humming and fussing with the stems, never knowing I was even there. More than once I nearly gave poor Henry, the sexton, a heart attack. And once I came in, climbed those pulpit stairs and stood there a long time, chattering aloud, before realizing that Greg, the organist, was also there in the same darkness, sitting at the organ in the balcony with a tiny light to read by, humming over the music for the following day. I smiled and waved, trying to assure both of us that I wasn't crazy, that I wasn't exactly talking to myself—but we knew each other pretty well by then. I'm sure that he was not convinced.

So there you have it for this one Thursday morning: Read as many voices as you can, sacred and secular, in as many languages and styles as you can and then, through prayer and practice (however peculiar), find your own voice and bravely use it.

Thanks for asking. With every good wish on your journey toward ministry, Victoria

P.S. This is my twentieth year. The process has not gotten easier. I am still afraid and I still feel that I am just beginning.

When the UUA's growth team invited twelve ministers to Louisville to talk about how congregations grow, they asked us a plain, beautiful question: What is the saving message that your congregation means to proclaim to the world? They were not asking us to tell how many members we have, how many in attendance, how many children in Religious Education, what kinds of classes, projects, and activities we offer. They were not asking us to say whether our congregations are primarily humanist or theist, pagan or liberal Christian, nor to talk about theology at all. We were not asked to discuss our governance models, long-range plans, the reporting relationships of staff and volunteers, our politics or our internal politics, our physical plants or square footage. They wanted to know what's underneath, and behind, and infusing all of that. They wanted us to tell them what we know by *heart*. In the context of a morning worship service, they invited us to answer one by one.

My colleagues spoke powerfully, almost tenderly. They spoke authentically, sometimes with cracking voices. They spoke with humility and pride, prophetically. When I finally took a breath and stepped into the circle, it was hard not to be intimidated. I thought of Sunday mornings in the sanctuary that is home to a people I love. I thought of worship there, week after week, year after year, and the saving message that touches the soul.

You are beloved of God.
The universe is glad to see you.
Everyone has a place at the table. Everyone is welcome.
Everyone belongs.
Everyone is accountable.
It is so easy to forget this. It is so easy to be reminded.

I'm not sure everyone in the congregation would choose to use this language, and yet I know that if the church has grown at all, deeper and wiser and better, as well as larger, it is because this intention, this good news, whether whispered or proclaimed, is heard in the Sunday services. It's spoken in the ways we hold our children and our teens, and in our work for peace and justice. It buzzes through the coffee hour and at the big band dance; it breathes through every note the choir sings, and in between the notes. It is visible in the art and in the very architecture. It echoes through every memorial, every service of union, every wedding, and in the Call to Worship and the Closing Words.

They've played that piece ten thousand times, sometimes haltingly and clumsily, a little out of tune, sometimes with breathtaking perfection. It is not an accident. It's purposeful. The openness, the friendliness, the order, the lack of order—all of this is how we practice our religion. When we are at our best, this message permeates everything we do, everything we say, every little thing, ten thousand encounters between the people and among them, and between each one and whatever it is that holds them in the hollow of its hand.

Worship that would touch the soul speaks with the integrity of the congregation's character. It speaks the truth, and tries to speak beautifully, even if that truth is hard. It speaks a saving message, and no matter how far it carries the people in the course of its hour, no matter how widely it ranges, it brings them safely home in time for the closing hymn, landing surely on the side of hope, the side of compassion and gratitude. It beckons always toward love and toward life.

Buzz

JOHN T. CRESTWELL JR.

It's Sunday morning. I am scurrying to get things organized, walking in and out of my office, up and down the aisles in the sanctuary, back and forth through the building. "Hey! How are you today?" I say to members who arrive early. My thoughts follow their usual pattern: "I need to put my sermon on the lectern. Is the chalice out? Are the microphones set up? Where's the Worship Associate? The choir sounds ready." Then I remember that I have a last-minute change to the hymn, so I head to the sanctuary again. "Hello, choir!" I chat with the music director for a bit and then head back to my office for a few seconds of meditation. On the way, I meet more people and chat with them, "Look at you! Hey! My man! Where's my hug? Thanks for letting me know that. I'll call you this week."

I get back to my office with seventeen minutes to spare. I leave the door open. I take a deep breath and stare out the window, watching people arrive, all shapes, sizes, and colors. I listen to little feet running down the hall, kids laughing; the sound of chatter is all around.

In this moment, I recall lyrics adapted from Doris Akers that speak to the electric energy of the gathered people: "There's a sweet, sweet Spirit in this place, and I know that it's the Spirit of our love."

I put on my robe and head to the door to give more hugs and greet folk. I wait as long as I can to go in to the service so I can make sure I speak to as many people as possible and also to make sure most are seated prior to worship.

As fewer and fewer people arrive, indicating to me that I need to begin the service, I am able for just a moment to hear an even sweeter sound. It is not as fragmented as the sounds heard from my office. This sound is polyphonic—made up of many sounds—but it is essentially one sound. It is a buzz. It has intonation, quality, and pitch. It's very light and gleeful; it is a happy sound. It is coming from many different places and from many different people, but it is a unified reverberation. It is the sound of hope, because Davies Memorial believes today that Beloved Community is more than just a utopian fantasy; it is the hum of expectation, because we feel the beauty that comes from worshiping in a racially diverse congregation. Ultimately, we feel the buzz of love, because we know as we come together each week that we are impacting and changing "the most segregated hour in the country."

The lovely buzz I hear at Davies before and after service came from great sweat, dedication, and tears. In 2003, we sought to intentionally become a racially diverse congregation. When I arrived in 2001, we were about 5 percent racially diverse, and after developing a plan of action, we are proud today that our Unitarian Universalist congregation is nearly 40 percent racially diverse. Our efforts were honored in 2007 by the Unitarian Universalist Association, when we were named a Breakthrough Congregation for our growth and diversity.

But being diverse is more than just statistics. The numbers that show progress are important, but what is behind it? Is it substantive? Is what we experience real and will it last, or is it contrived and the result of having an African-American minister? I've pondered this about Davies as we've grown more racially diverse.

The answer to these questions came to me several months ago when I was at church on a Saturday for an activity and witnessed what our work is all about. I was staring out the window while others were busy, and I saw the most amazing thing. I witnessed a forty-something African-American man sitting outside chatting with an eighty-something European-American man. They sat there for quite some time, and I could tell they were having a good conversation. They were more than cordial, more than tolerant. They fully respected each other's worth and dignity and were enjoying each other's company. I remember saying to myself, "That's what it's all about." It's about right relationship, building real associations with those who are very different from us. It's about expanding our sphere of influence so that we begin to attract different kinds of people and experiences into our lives. It's about challenging our suppositions in life and being willing to have that conversation with a new person, and trying something innovative in worship that will attract various ethnicities to our church. It's about embracing our cultural differences as a virtue.

Having a multiracial congregation is a wonderful gift. However, Davies' buzz comes from our ability to develop solid relationships with newcomers, members, friends, and their children. The feeling people get when they come to Davies is the result of our intention to be welcoming—our sincere desire to welcome the stranger. A recent visitor to our congregation, Brian Hedges, sent me an email that describes the visitor's experience. He is part of a group contemplating starting a UU congregation in Rappahannock, Virginia, and is interested in building a multiracial church.

> After reading Rev. John Crestwell's book, *The Charge of the Chalice*, I decided to attend the service at Davies Memorial. . . . I wasn't at all prepared for what I experienced. This fellowship is indeed diverse, with about 40 percent black and 60 percent white membership. I have never experienced a service with the joy and energy present at this one. . . . Let me tell you, if you haven't heard "Lean on Me" sung to piano, keyboard, trumpet and percussion, you haven't really heard it yet.
>
> Rev. Crestwell talked about the tension between pluralism and assimilation. To what extent do we celebrate our diversity versus demanding that minorities conform to the majority culture? He said that we must honor each other "not despite our differences but because of our differences." He went on to say that although every church claims to be

welcoming, many in fact are not welcoming to outsiders; and that there is a new multi-cultural multi-ethnic paradigm in this country. Unitarian Universalism is mostly behind the times in this respect, following an assimilation model that asks people to conform to UU's dominant white culture if they want to join. . . . We must look at racial, theological, accessibility, sexual orientation, and musical diversity. We need to do this to live out our faith and also so as not to be left behind. . . .

Before I drove up for this service I knew intellectually that a diverse fellowship was critically important to me. . . . As I sat participating in the service I realized all the same things, but in a new way. I could feel that this was being alive, this was having energy; this was being fully engaged in creating and living something beautiful.

The electricity, the buzz that is in the air at Davies comes from developing a congregational consciousness centered in authentic ministry, and real ministry is soul work that challenges us at our spiritual core, asking us to be more than we are and to do more to lift up the human condition. Soul work asks that we be fully present in the modern world, to participate and not hibernate from the realities that plague us, and to be open to the opportunities that are before us.

Buzz—this feeling of energy—is not something you can buy. It is not something you can fake. It comes from authenticity and from people experiencing transformation in their lives. Authenticity and transformation are not possible only in multiracial congregations. But for Davies, the experience of creating a beloved community that is authentic and multiracial has been a catalyst for transformation.

We came to realize that multicultural worship changes us for the better in very profound ways. In my years with Davies, I have learned that several things must be considered if a congregation hopes for this kind of ministry:

❖ *Develop a multicultural model.* Congregations need to live out the true meaning of our Principles, which remind us to think and act intentionally about what it means to "lift up the worth and dignity of all."

❖ *Reflect the demographics of the community in the congregation.* An authentic Unitarian Universalism will shape itself to the needs and desires of the local community it serves, transforming its ministry to meet those needs.

❖ *Have persons of color in leadership positions that reflect the racially diverse outcome desired.* We must reflect what we are and wish to be. We live our goal before the desired end has become manifest. So if we desire a racially diverse congregation, we employ a qualified racially diverse staff that shows every person present in the church what the future will look like.

❖ *Demonstrate diversity in every facet of the ministry, such as leadership, websites, brochures and other publicity, pictures of members, and music.* When visitors and members come to your church, they must see what you are but also what you are becoming. If you are not diverse, but they see in all of your marketing, administration, and programming that you are working toward that goal, they will stay. Many will join because they share your hope to move beyond monoculturalism to multiculturalism. Highlight your congregation's dream in every aspect of its ministry.

❖ *Racial diversity will not happen by accident; it must be pursued intentionally.* This does not mean that spirit will not confound us in some modest or extraordinary way on the journey. However, the traditional white culture of Unitarian Universalism is pervasive, and without a deeper understanding of what we are and where we are going, we will find ourselves doing the same things over again and achieving the same results. Developing a strategic plan will help focus your congregation so you can institute programs that restructure attitudes and perceptions that block the spirit from moving in new and exciting ways. A plan with specific means and an end goal will help expand your congregation's consciousness in new directions, preventing a reversion to the status quo. *Intentional* also means deliberate, planned, and calculated, requiring you to be dogged in your approach and execution.

The buzz at Davies is not unlike that in many of our congregations. All loving congregations have a buzz in some way, shape, or form. What I've outlined is not exclusive to a racially diverse church. However, the process at Davies has transformed the lives of many in the church, including me. I grew up in an all-black neighborhood and went to all African-American schools, with the exception of seminary. When I came to our faith, my first vision was to build an all-black UU Church—that's all I knew! However, one Sunday I saw something that instantly transformed me. As I looked in the pulpit, I saw four girls: my daughter, a Native-American girl, and two girls of European ancestry singing "Spirit of Life" together. It was the cutest picture in the world! I saw a vision of the Beloved Community and my heart was touched deeply. The words of John Newton came to mind then: "I once was lost but now am found, was blind but now I see!" I knew then that multicultural community was better for me and a goal I would set my heart to.

If you believe in your heart that developing a diverse congregation will enhance your congregation's buzz even more, then I leave you with a few questions to ponder:

How can you transform your administration, worship service, religious education, programming, and marketing to be more inclusive and pluralistic for this changing time in America? Are you ready to accept that some things must evolve so that our faith can survive and thrive in this new century? What are you willing to do to "be the change we wish to see"?

These are the hard questions, but I have great faith that in this new age of hope, Unitarian Universalism will manifest its greatness so that those who yearn for our brand of religion might find us worthy of their time, talent, and treasure. Let it be so!

WELCOMING

PETER MORALES

Every single Sunday morning they come. On a typical Sunday, our congregations receive thousands of people who have come to see if they might find their spiritual home. We don't know precisely how many come, but my best estimate is about four to five thousand a week. That means that our congregations receive on the order of a quarter of a million visitors a year. In one year, we receive far more visitors than we have members.

Think about your own congregation for a moment. Let's say yours is a pretty typically sized congregation of 150 adult members. You'd have to receive on average only 3 visitors per week to get 150 per year. Now stop and think about how many visitors come just on Easter and Christmas Eve.

I make it a practice on Sunday mornings to stand outside before each service to welcome people (although I take a lot of teasing when people find me greeting inside during a Colorado snowstorm). I began this practice when I first settled at Jefferson Unitarian Church. As the new minister, I wanted to greet and get to know the people in our congregation. However, it quickly became a spiritual discipline for me. As the weeks went by, I was amazed at the number of first-time visitors I encountered. As the months and years went by, this practice of greeting, like any good spiritual discipline, changed me profoundly.

Week after week, I met people who came to our congregation longing for a spiritual home. As we became more aware of this steady stream of visitors, we started to pay attention to what visitors experienced on Sunday morning. We began to pay attention to the things we did to make them feel welcome or not welcome. Frankly, we were appalled.

Like most churches, we had a warm, friendly, welcoming self-image. The truth was that, when we looked at what the typical visitor experienced, we fell far short of being the church we thought we were. We had fallen gradually into a lot of bad habits. We had unintentionally created barriers. I still remember hearing a relatively new member serving on our membership committee say, "We had to fight our way into this church." Ouch! That really stung.

So we started changing some simple things. We began to practice hospitality; we intentionally worked at becoming the warm church we wanted to be. As the years went on, we kept making changes, always trying to see ourselves as a newcomer does. We soon became one of the fastest-growing churches in our movement. And we were transformed, spiritually transformed, by our practice of hospitality. The spiritual practice of deep hospitality made us more aware of others, more sensitive, more empathetic, and less self-centered. When we listened, really listened, to people joining our church, the programmatic implications were profound.

The single greatest issue that will determine our future as a religious movement is how visitors feel in our church. The single most important thing we can do for our movement, and the single most important gift we can give to those coming to us, is to make visitors feel like our congregation is their spiritual home.

This issue is not really one of outreach. It is not really a matter of institutional health. It is not a question of making a few cosmetic changes on Sunday morning. It most certainly is not a question of growing for the sake of growing, because it is not about numbers. It's about people. When we focus on people and their real needs, the numbers will take care of themselves. The issue of religious hospitality is ultimately a moral and spiritual issue—and how we respond to this spiritual challenge will determine the future of each one of our congregations and the future of the Unitarian Universalist movement.

Religious hospitality is the moral equivalent of feeding the hungry and giving shelter to the homeless. The people coming to us are spiritually hungry and religiously homeless. But let me back up for a minute. Why are so many people coming to us? What are they looking for, and, just as important, what are they *not* looking for? If we are to be spiritually relevant, we must understand the cultural, historical, emotional, and spiritual context in which we live. It has changed dramatically in the last generation, and it will change at blinding speed in the next twenty years. The new people coming to our churches arrive with a deep hunger. Often, they don't know what it is. They experience this hunger as a vague emptiness, as something missing in their lives. What is going on?

Americans today are the most isolated people in human history. That is a bold statement. But consider some breathtaking research in the field of social psychology. A study published in the June 2006 *American Sociological Review* shows a decline in close relationships so large and so rapid that the data shocked sociologists. The findings were so shocking, in fact, that they were picked up by publications like the *New York Times*.

The study was essentially a repetition of one done in 1985. Both interviewed participants about the number of people in whom they confide personal information, and both asked participants a number of questions about their confidants. By asking the same questions asked in 1985, they could track changes.

For example, in 1985, the modal response (the response given most often) to the question about the number of confidants was three. In 2004, the modal response was zero. The percentage of people who said that they had no one with whom they could confide jumped from 10 percent in 1985 to 24.6 percent in 2004. That means that in just 20 years, the percentage of people who said they have no one to talk to went from one person in ten to one out of every four.

According to the study, almost half of all Americans now have either no one or only one person with whom they can discuss important matters. This number has almost doubled in twenty years. If a person has only one confidant, chances are that the one confidant is his or her partner or spouse, indicating that ties beyond the nuclear family are disappearing.

People who have either no confidant or only one confidant have inadequate support. These results indicate that in a single generation, the percentage of people with inadequate social support has gone from a quarter of the population (bad enough) to almost half the population. And the biggest decline has been in the relationships that link us to our neighbors and our community.

These are not dull, abstract numbers. They are a cry of isolation, of pain, of loneliness. Americans are far lonelier than they were a generation ago. Many of us are lonely, and all of us are surrounded by lonely people. Loneliness is among us like an invisible epidemic.

We have unwittingly created a culture that rips apart human ties outside the household. Causes include our high level of mobility, the erosion of neighborhoods, and the isolating character of the automobile. Television and the Internet, while they appear to connect people, actually impede intimate interpersonal engagement. Our culture has long celebrated the individual at the expense of the community. More than a quarter of all American households are now single-person households. The list goes on and on. The combined effect is that we face an emotional and spiritual crisis.

We need one another. You and I are relational creatures. We are hardwired that way. It is in relationship that we become fully human. It is in relationship that we find fulfillment. Only when we transcend our individuality do we touch the divine. All of the great religious traditions teach the importance of our connection to one another.

We have all seen horrible pictures of starving people in third-world countries. These pictures touch our hearts; our sympathy is instantaneous. If we could take pictures of the souls of Americans, we would see that they are shriveled, starved for deep, honest, authentic, intimate human contact. The statistics I have cited represent spiritual and emotional starvation that is growing at an alarming rate. These are the people who are coming to church every Sunday. They seek religious community. They seek relationships of depth, meaning, and purpose.

They are also seeking to join with others to make a difference in the world. In the past several years, we have noticed a definite trend in our congregation that I suspect is typical. In our new member class, we ask people to tell us what they are most interested in exploring. The options include spiritual practices such as meditation groups, the liberal study of religion, social action, and articulating their own spirituality. In the past several years, in classes involving several hundred people, we've seen a clear trend toward social action. People come to church in order to give of themselves, to get involved, to make a difference.

Upon further reflection, of course, we see that our need for close relationships and our need to join with others to make a difference are aspects of the same human longing. We have a deep need to be in intimate relationships. We also have a need to be in relationship with those beyond our immediate circle. People feel, although they cannot always articulate, the inescapable connection between loving personal relationships and social justice, equity, and compassion. They come to church seeking both. They realize, if only vaguely, that when they connect with others in compassion and commitment, they are touching the holy.

While it is crucial to understand what the people who come to our congregations are seeking, it is equally important to understand what they are not seeking. Too often we offer people what we mistakenly think they want instead of what they need.

People are not coming to us to find out if they agree with us. The needs that bring them to our doors are not intellectual and cognitive. We too often give people a stone when they come seeking bread. In fact, visitors are not even coming to find out what we think. Because we live in a virtual era, most of the first-time visitors who walk up the sidewalk on Sunday morning are not really visiting for the first time. They might be making their first physical visit, but most of them have already visited virtually. They have been to our websites. In fact, I am constantly surprised by how many visitors have already read my sermons on our website. They may have been to UUA.org or to sites such as beliefnet.com. People who visit us today already know that they are in broad agreement with us. When was the last time someone came to your church mistakenly thinking they were going to get Bible study and traditional Christianity? When we talk to these people primarily about what we believe, we are having the wrong conversation. If they didn't share our basic beliefs and values, they wouldn't have come in the first place. They do not know if church will offer them an escape from isolation through connection and the opportunity to make a difference in the world.

Visitors are not in flight from fundamentalism. Very few of our visitors have left conservative churches. The fact that we are at the opposite end of the theological spectrum from the religious right does not, by itself, cut much ice. They are not running away from something; they are coming to fill a deep need. These people do not need to be told what we are not; they need to know if they belong.

The fundamental question in the minds and hearts of visitors is not, "Do I agree with these people?" The fundamental question is affective and tribal: "Are these my people?" Visitors want to know if there is a place for them, if they will feel accepted, if they can forge deep friendships. Parents want to feel that their children will be safe and will be taught values like tolerance and sharing. They want to know if we are walking our talk in the community. They want to know if they can be themselves, and if they will be accepted for who they are.

If we are going to make a difference in the lives of people, and if we are going to have impact in the wider world, we must learn to minister to a new America. Where shall we begin?

The initial work, as always, is spiritual. We must begin with awareness and compassion. We begin by truly opening our hearts. When we open our hearts to those coming to us and to the pain of their isolation, we immediately want to reach out. That, after all, is what love is; reaching out is how love expresses itself. Opening our hearts also means—and we too often forget this crucial element— that we have to be willing to be changed by our new relationships.

When love and awareness guide us, we realize that to ignore the pain and the needs of the thousands of people who walk into our churches every week is morally wrong. To ignore the visitor is not bad manners. It is immoral.

Some people think that the desire to grow our churches is somehow self-serving, others that it is in conflict with authentic spirituality. They consider the desire to grow to be competitive and materialistic. In reality, the opposite is true. Churches where the people truly make room in their hearts and where love thrives are churches that will grow over time. For most churches, growth over time is the single best measure of their spiritual health.

Visitors who come looking for a spiritual home pick up on spiritual health immediately. If a church is indifferent to a newcomer, it feels cold. Visitors sense right away whether that is the atmosphere, or if the congregation feels like a club run by and for the old-timers. Think of your own experience. Recall a time when you have walked into a room filled with strangers. How long does it take you to sense whether you are welcome? How long does it take to discern whether the people are happy? How long does it take to gauge the energy level? Not very long at all. We human beings are very sensitive to the emotional tone of a room.

We too often think that growing our congregations is a matter of technique, that if we develop a checklist of things to do and make sure we do them all, growth will magically follow. The following practices are things we can do to grow. But they are simply meant to be tools—the key is that we carry them out with genuine openness and compassion.

❖ Create relationships immediately. The first few minutes are important. How a person feels when he or she first walks in our door is critical and cannot be left to chance. Someone, preferably the minister if there is one, must greet newcomers personally. I have heard some ministerial colleagues say they don't feel comfortable doing this. I say, do it anyway! After a couple of times, it will seem natural. Make sure the friendliest extroverts in the congregation are waiting to follow up with name tags, introductions to others, answers to questions, and other essentials. At my congregation, I want every visitor to receive at least three warm greetings in the first ten minutes. The time after the service is equally important. Start a conversation. Ask the newcomer what brought them. Communicating to the visitor that we are genuinely glad to see them and that we hope they will return is essential.

❖ Feed their souls. In every survey I have seen that asks members why they keep coming and why they are committed to church, "community" comes up more times than all other responses combined. That has profound implications for our activities as a spiritual community, from worship to social action to religious education to pastoral care. Even those activities that seem least interactive, like silent meditation, need a communal component.

The hunger to connect is so powerful today that we need to be intentional about bringing it to all aspects of life. For example, some element of deep sharing on the theme of the worship service by a member of the congregation is central to our worship. We have multiple opportunities for our members simply to be together at events, such as fellowship dinners and lunches for older members.

People also come to us to connect with their entire selves. For instance, music has a profound effect on people, touching something deep in ourselves and in each other. When we share our different musical traditions, we open the door to diversity. At First Jefferson, we always close the service with everyone holding hands. Touch, like music, creates powerful bonds.

❖ Nurture the connections. We have long known that the best predictor of whether someone will become a long-term member of a church is the number of friendships he or she forms in the first six months. We cannot simply leave this to chance. Someone has to nurture relationships and help each new person find his or her place. Who will do this depends, of course, on the size and unique composition of each congregation. It might be a member who is a leader. It might be the minister. In a large church, it might be a paid staff person whose job is to facilitate these connections. Whoever does it—and it will be the work of the many and not the few—needs to genuinely get to know new people and find out what they love to do or have always wanted to try. One person may need meditation or a small group. The next might want to work on environmental issues, another to help with pastoral care. What is important is helping people participate in something they will find meaningful. It does not mean getting a new member to fill an empty slot on a dysfunctional committee.

❖ Put them to work. We often forget that one of our fundamental needs is to contribute. There was a time when I actively discouraged new members from joining a committee. I did not want some committee chair to grab them. Instead, I wanted to give them time to explore the variety of groups and activities available. I was so wrong. I soon learned that most people want to get involved right away, especially those with a passion for social justice. We ask members to commit to Sunday morning volunteer work, such as ushering, making coffee, or helping in the nursery, on the day they join. And, of course, they meet a lot of new people this way.

❖ Don't get stuck. Things change. We must not get trapped into implementing a number of welcoming techniques and then just falling into a new set of habits. A few years ago, my congregation produced a DVD showcasing our welcoming practices as part of the first UU University. It was sent all over the country, and we still get questions about our practices. We're a little embarrassed, though, that we no longer do some of the things on the video. Some didn't work, so we changed them. We also had new and better ideas. The important thing is to be sensitive to people and what works for them.

If I could change one thing about our movement, I would have every parish minister greet every single person who comes to church.

I would also have every single member greet people alongside the minister at least once. I truly believe that this practice could transform our movement. If everyone could meet these people, could shake their hands and chat for a little while, we would see clearly the need, the longing, the pain, and the desire to be part of something that transcends banality and materialism. These people share our values. They share our outlook. And they are looking for a home.

While speaking to a large group at a UU conference, I asked everyone in the audience of lay leaders to raise a hand if they had ever visited another UU congregation. Almost all the hands went up. I then asked them to leave their hands up if they had ever felt ignored while visiting one of our churches. Almost all the hands stayed up. Over the years, I've repeated this shtick a number of times, and the result is always the same. I have had the same experience of being ignored many times. It is very sad, and terribly discouraging. It is as though, unwittingly and with no malice, we ignore people who are starving and homeless.

The possibilities are breathtaking, if only we open our hearts to these people, if only we dare to reach out and engage them. We can touch hundreds of thousands of lives. Imagine our churches re-energized, vital, growing by leaps and bounds, just as my church and dozens of others have grown. And when we allow our churches to grow, they become more powerful forces for compassion, for peace, for environmental stewardship, and for justice.

It all begins—all of it—with opening our hearts. It begins with a smile, a handshake, and a simple conversation. We can save souls from isolation and meaninglessness. We can make a difference in the world. We can transform our movement. Transforming lives, healing the world, revitalizing our faith, one relationship at a time.

It all begins next Sunday. They are coming by the thousands.

Innovation

CHRISTINE ROBINSON

We expect and enjoy innovation in our world. We like our new toys and conveniences, "improved" products sell, and the latest always seems best. Religious institutions can not ignore cultural bias toward innovation, especially if they want to remain attractive to young people and to people who are new to church culture. Furthermore, life in this rapidly changing world requires us to change even if we don't want to. Neighborhoods change, zoning codes change, who is free to volunteer and who enters religious leadership changes, even climate changes. Congregational growth is a welcome change that requires innovation. Congregational shrinkage is an unwelcome change that also requires innovation. Congregational aging is an inevitable change, and that requires innovation too. Wherever we turn, something is changing, and we have to ask ourselves how to respond.

Whenever I'm tempted to bemoan changing conditions, I think of the wonderful saying, "In the bottom of God's pocket is change." This saying expresses the positive attitude toward change required to be an innovator or a leader in an innovative institution. Not only is change inevitable in our lives, it is holy. It invites the new into the world, makes us cocreators, and reminds us of what we deeply value. We know that things change, and we believe that change is good.

To make some of these observations about change concrete, here is just one example of the innovative approaches we have tried at the congregation I serve. First Unitarian in Albuquerque, New Mexico, is a large church with a small sanctuary, which we have stuffed with chairs to the point that most worship innovations, especially those requiring the congregation to move around, are impossible. However, one oddity of our sanctuary is that we have a lot of open space between the platform that is our chancel and the front windows. If we cleared out some clutter, perhaps we could move people through there. Last All Souls' Sunday, we hung pictures of deceased church members and church members' loved ones on that wall. There was even a pet section. During the service, we proposed a walking meditation and invited everyone in the congregation to get up and walk slowly past the photographs. The experience was quite moving, even for those folks who didn't know anyone in the pictures. For those of us who did, or who actually had a loved one the wall, it was powerful and healing, putting sorrow in a larger, loving context. As we planned this service, we were aware of the risks. What if people didn't want to bother to get up? What if the experience was too powerful, and everyone dissolved in tears? What if we'd misjudged the time it would take? What if it seemed merely sentimental or depressing? We discussed those questions at length, and the end result was worth the anxiety. Not only did we develop a very effective, repeatable All Souls' service, but we also started to think outside our sanctuary box for other kinds of worship innovations.

We're faced with a conundrum: Congregations need to be innovative, but they have great difficulty with innovation. If you search the web for "innovation, ministry," the only sites you find are those about government ministries! If we are going to be innovative leaders in churches, we have to understand why we struggle with associating the two.

The church, as a category of institution, plays a fundamentally conservative role in society. I mean this in the best sense of the word. Religious institutions play an important role in society as conservators of values, of the wisdom of the past, and of traditions. We tend to turn to religious institutions when we want stability in our lives, not when we want change. For example, at times of fundamental change—marriage, birth, death—we turn instinctively to the comforting spaces and rituals of conserving institutions: churches, synagogues, temples. This especially fits the fixed theology of many conservative religious institutions, which teach a truth received in the past that is forever to be believed and preserved. However, even theologically liberal institutions have a conservative function and are rarely as "out there" as other kinds of liberal institutions.

Members of more liberal denominations tend to assume that their movement's willingness to be theologically innovative translates to being comfortable with all kinds of innovation, but this is not always the case. Actually, it is more likely that theologically conservative congregations will succeed in being innovative. Think about contemporary music in worship or about worship times other than Sunday morning. The Catholics started down that road thirty years ago and were followed by theologically conservative Protestants.

These changes puzzle liberals, who feel that they should be on the cutting edge of everything, but the explanation is simple. First, both individuals and groups are more willing to accept change if they believe that it will help them accomplish an important shared mission. Second, they are more willing to try a new expression of their faith if they have and share a strong core of beliefs and practices that provide stability in times of change. Third, they will be better able to carry out change if they are willing to trust a strong leader. Catholics and Evangelical Protestants have all three of these factors on their side. They believe that using contemporary music in their worship will reach "a new generation for Christ," and that Saturday afternoon worship times will get more people to church. They can articulate the core of their faith and are confident that they share that core with their congregation. And they are, generally, willing followers of strong leaders.

Liberal congregations usually have to manage change without any of these factors on their side. They are often suspicious of a strong sense of mission or a shared core of faith, fearful that they will eliminate diversity of thought or limit individual rights. They are usually unwilling followers and don't care for strong leaders. Theologically liberal congregations still have to change and can be innovative, however. It's just harder.

Other factors make innovation difficult in religious institutions, whether liberal or conservative. Innovation is costly. For example, the innovative mindset needs nurturing by sabbaticals, conferences, and books, and the time to read and ponder them. Chronically overstressed and underfunded congregations might consider these sources of nurturing luxuries, refusing to fund them, and then wonder why their leaders are dull and unexciting, and why their programs lack innovative thinking.

In addition, innovative programs often require up-front expenditures, with the risk that they will not be recovered. Financial stress can create group dynamics which are contemptuous of risk taking and innovative leadership. Some ministers, for instance, are unkind to innovative or risk-taking colleagues, and some denominations are often suspicious of innovative congregations and their leaders. Most churches, especially smaller ones, think of themselves as "family," and as in a family, one person who is unhappy with a proposed change can hold veto power.

Vitally important when it comes to innovation in worship, part of the mission of every congregation is to help people experience and develop their spirituality. The experience of spirituality is, for most people, one of surrendering, of feeling both vulnerable and taken care of. To experience these feelings, we must have a sense of safety and familiarity. Only when we feel safe can we drop our usual defenses and relax into a spiritual mood, open to the moment and open to the divine. When we are part of a worshiping congregation, the sights and smells, the feel of the pew, the familiar sounds and songs signal to our wary brains, "It's okay here. You can relax and let go. You can worship."

Of course, those signals vary according to past experience. If you are a Native American Pueblo dweller, the sound of drums may help create a spiritual mood. If you worship in a traditional New England church, the sound of drums will probably chase away every spiritual possibility. If you have been part of a contemporary worship service, you might need to clap and sway from side to side to "get in the mood." If you are a traditional Jew, swaying forward and backward will help you pray. If you are a Quaker or a Zen Buddhist, stillness and quiet will help move you to the inner place of prayer. Because we human beings can be spiritual in almost any environment, once we feel safe and familiar, innovation—especially in worship and worship spaces—must be managed carefully. And many religious leaders have discovered that even innovation outside the mechanics of worship —opening the church to the homeless several nights a week, for instance—will shatter the sense of safety and openness some people need to feel spiritual.

Finally, religious institutions may not recognize the incentive to innovate as, for example, commercial enterprises do. Congregations already have impressive customer loyalty (although that has eroded in this generation), so innovation can seem unnecessary or not worth the trouble and expense. Congregations derive significant funds from their endowments—the present gifts of past loyalty—that could be used to fund the costs of risk and innovation. Too often financially embattled congregations use their endowments conservatively. Their endowments subsidize a congregation whose status quo is not self-sustaining. If some of this wealth was invested in innovation instead, the congregation might break this cycle.

Contemplating all the factors stacked against innovation in congregations, and especially liberal congregations, might discourage some readers. The creative reader, however, will think, "Well, we'll just have to be intentional." Innovation in church requires balancing comfort and challenge in the congregation, especially in the worship services. Endowments and other money from the past can be dedicated to innovation rather than to funding ongoing costs of ministry. Encourage denominational officials to notice whether they are being too hard on innovative leaders and to try to curb negativity toward them. Innovative leaders need to pay extra attention to "bringing people along" with their plans and attaching their ideas to the mission and ministry of the congregation if they want their ideas to come to fruition.

At First Unitarian, most of the older adults in our congregation do not use YouTube, and we'd never try to get congregational news out that way. However, we do post short sermons to YouTube, which limits videos to five minutes, and we occasionally offer sermons in four- and five-minute segments to make this bit of outreach possible. We explain to our older adults what YouTube is and why it is important to younger people. We thank them for putting up with four-segment sermons and for being a part of this outreach to new generations. In other words, we attach this uncomfortable innovation to our mission. We sometimes show YouTube segments at coffee hour, so they can "get the picture," and we've shown some of our interested adults how to use YouTube, podcasting, blogging, and Facebook (yes, our church has a Facebook page with about eighty members), and how they can access print, audio, and video copies of sermons from the church website. We offer this small service to our older members to entice them as far into the digital age as they are able to go. But even those who are not able are glad to see the young people in the congregation.

We ministers have noticed that, these days, young visitors to our congregation come with the question, "Can I find a place for myself here?" They have already answered the question, "Do I believe what they teach here?" by watching the sermon videos. The very fact that those videos are there says to younger seekers, "This church is a part of my world. I'd be safe there." The young people who come to us bring us their energy, their babies, their "take it for granted" multicultural selves, and their confirmation that our church has something to offer the future. The costs of the video camera, the computer and software, the upgraded website, and increased volunteer complexity have been worth every penny we've spent!

It's a rare congregation that doesn't want to grow but an even rarer one that really counts the costs of growing. Members in growing churches often complain that they don't "know anybody anymore." They do so whether the church grows from 80 to 120 members or from 500 to 650 members. (It must be human nature!) Leaders in growing churches are more likely to bemoan how much more work there is. It's not just that more bodies create more work; the very structures that served a smaller congregation must be reworked. The family-sized church that finds itself with three new families with small children must now create a nursery. The program-sized church that has taken in one hundred new members needs a more effective way to govern their larger congregation. The minister who has advocated for a staff to help with the workload suddenly finds herself with a new job—the job of supervising and nurturing someone else's work.

Generally, the increase in membership fills the sanctuary and the classrooms long before it fills church coffers, so innovation must be done with limited resources or major risk taking. Growth sometimes plateaus because the growth spurt makes new work for everyone, and staying at the new size requires restructuring, which is another massive undertaking. If laypersons, staff, and ministers can't muster the energy to make those changes, the church quickly falls back to the more comfortable, smaller size. But graceful church downsizing requires the same extraordinary dedication, and it's just as necessary for the health of the church.

Successful innovation requires four core strengths: analysis, creativity, risk, and the ability to manage change. Analyzing the situation means understanding what exactly is happening. Creativity is the ability to come up with new ideas and to solve problems in sometimes unconventional ways. However, creative thinking can feel risky, and implementing creative ideas requires willingness to take risk. Finally, creative innovation requires the ability to manage people's often negative response to change.

We don't innovate for innovation's sake; we innovate to solve problems or create opportunities in accordance with our mission. Successful innovation arises from a response to conditions, and we have to first analyze those conditions.

At one time in my church, noticeably fewer people were signing the membership book. One response to this problem could have been to create a catchy billboard to advertise the church. But a systematic thinker did some analysis. Looking over our guest book, she ascertained that we had had as many visitors to the church as ever. Further analysis indicated that we had many people on our path to membership, some of whom had been on that path for a long time. After asking a few of them to tell us about their relationship to the church, we learned that many thought they were already members because the materials they had been given were misleading. Others had grown frustrated with what they called "hoop jumping" and had lost interest. With that information, we applied our creative energy not to billboards but to our Path to Membership program. People started joining the church again.

Everyone is capable of creativity, although it comes more easily to some than to others, and it's easier in some situations than in others. Innovative leaders create conditions within which they and their teams will think outside the box. The well-known rules of brainstorming offer a basic outline for free-flowing creativity. Brainstorming works best in a group, where people's ideas can build on one another's. Most people have to be given explicit permission to say the first zany thing that comes to mind, but that's what creativity takes. There is no evaluation of or sniping at ideas during brainstorming, so people can feel safe taking risks. Brainstorming works when you're being creative on your own too. You can write down every idea and delay evaluation until you've finished.

These guidelines are useful beyond the occasional brainstorming session. They form the backbone of an innovative culture. Leadership and staff training should emphasize the importance of listening first and evaluating later. An innovative congregation will be a permission-giving culture: the general attitude that new ideas are good, that we try out new programs, that someone with an idea to implement will be given a hearing and, if the idea is sound, allowed to proceed.

Creative thinking outside the box is enhanced by getting outside the box. Travel, conferences, sabbaticals, wide reading, and even daily meditation time foster creativity. Religious leaders who read mystery novels, surf the web, attend the occasional business or science conference, notice what their interfaith colleagues are doing, and give themselves unstructured quiet time each day are more likely to be more creative than those who keep their nose to the grindstone and rarely leave the safe confines of their own congregation. Congregational leaders who go to denominational conferences, visit other congregations when they travel, and engage in a spiritual practice are also likely to be more creative and more open to innovation.

Leaders in small denominations, especially, must get out of their denominational neighborhoods. To be innovative in worship, leaders should experience worship in other places. This is not easy, especially for clergy, since so much worship happens on Sunday mornings when clergy are working. But other faiths hold worship services at other times of the weekend, and more and more, innovative churches hold worship beyond Sunday morning. Conference worship services are generally innovative, and every clergy person with worship responsibilities should include worshiping in other congregations in their sabbatical plans. Laypersons should be encouraged to visit other churches of their faith when they travel. If their minister tells them it is important and listens to their stories when they return, they are more likely to do so. After all, the manager of your local grocery store has been visiting the competition and knows exactly what they are doing and how it is working.

Let me share an example of an idea I encountered while on sabbatical. During a visit to a Presbyterian colleague's congregation, I experienced a lively, engaging offering. Most UUs pay their pledge by mail or bank draft, a practice with such a wonderful effect on our cash flow that I wouldn't dream of changing it. But when the offering plates would come around in Albuquerque, mostly only children and visitors put anything in, making the offering seem meager and the congregation appear to lack generosity because giving was hidden. In contrast, this Presbyterian church invited people to empty their pockets and purses of coins—just coins—and announced that all those coins would be going to the local food bank. What a joyful noise that offering made! As the downright heavy plates went by me, I did the math and understood why this church appeared on the "silver donors" list of so many good causes around town! Better still, everyone participated in this high-spirited offering, although most of them probably also paid their pledge by mail and bank draft.

I brought this idea home and tried it out. It was a huge hit, and we suddenly had about $500 a month to give to good causes in our city. But nothing is perfect. Remember how very conservative people are when it comes to changes in their worship service. The music lovers grumbled that all that coin rattling disturbed their musical experience. Now, one could throw up one's hands in disgust over such bellyaching in the face of a worthy cause, but that wouldn't be productive. Better to earnestly agree that it's hard to listen to a recorder quintet when all around you is the clinking of charitable giving. That sympathy brought out everyone's creativity. Turns out all we had to do to solve this problem was purchase deeper baskets and pad them well. We also asked the music director to arrange the offering music from the louder end of the spectrum for a while.

All the creativity in the world is useless if a leader or a group can't handle the risks involved in trying something new. Congregations are a hard environment to take risks in, and denominations are often worse. National leadership that wants innovative congregations and religious leaders will make grant money available and make it easy for amateur grant writers to apply. A creative minister who can say to the congregation, "I've got a great idea, I know how to help you do it, and someone from headquarters liked it so much, they offered to give us half the money we need," is more than halfway to implementing that great idea.

Not all creative ideas work. But an innovative culture within a denomination will honor the learnings of failure as well as the glamour of success. An innovative collegial culture will eagerly ask participants in failed experiments what they got out of their experience and what they would do differently, and not just listen to the success stories. When innovators are allowed to make midcourse corrections and tweak their grants and proposals, everyone benefits.

When taking risks in innovation, it is helpful to have a strong shared mission. Those who must gather their courage to take the risk of proposing and implementing innovative ideas are bolstered if they can say, "We're doing this because it is a part of our mission." One of the signature initiatives for which First Unitarian Church in Albuquerque is known required taking significant risks.

The congregation outgrew its sanctuary several years before we could afford a new one, so we videotaped sermons and used the recorded sermons as the centerpiece of a small-group worship in our Social Hall. A few experiments seemed to work, and then the innovative lightbulb went on. If we could create a small-group worship service in our own Social Hall using these videos, we could do the same in the small towns that dot New Mexico—towns where there were not enough UUs for an independent congregation. If we could provide the sermon, these little groups could focus on doing the rest of their worship service well, on having a covenant group, and on providing religious education programming. As the large church in our state, we have long felt some responsibility to nurture Unitarian Universalism, and part of our mission is to "promote the wider understanding of our purposes and principles." The board, staff, and congregation were intrigued.

Knowing that our staff couldn't go out and organize groups that were thirty to three hundred miles from Albuquerque, we asked the Fund for Unitarian Universalism and the UUA together for a grant to pay a staff person for eighteen months to do this work and create a model for other congregations. We were given the funding. Would we be able to do what we hoped to do? It felt risky. It could have been a huge waste of money. If we couldn't do what we hoped to do, we would experience a very public failure. The congregation was excited about this project, but failure would impact their morale. They, like the funding panel, had put their trust in this idea and in the people who were going to implement it.

At the end of the eighteen months, we'd organized two branches that were great successes. Our organizer had been to four other towns, but it takes a while to cultivate interest in most places. When his job ran out, the Albuquerque staff took on the two branches and quit organizing. It was a mistake. We should have applied for a three-year grant. Our branches struggled, and no new branches were started. It wasn't exactly a failure, but it sure wasn't thriving. After twenty-two months, we knew we had to do something. We had not spent all the money we'd been given, so we confessed our situation to our grantors and asked for permission to use the remainder to hire another staff person. We learned a lot from that mistake.

We can analyze a situation, respond creatively, and risk implementing it to produce innovation. However, we also need to bone up on our ability to manage change. Generally speaking, most people don't like change, especially in church. As one wag said, "Most people spell the word *change* l-o-s-s." Here are some thoughts about managing change to help creative ideas from risk-taking leaders succeed:

❖ Change should always implement mission. Convincing people to change should start with a reminder of the mission, particularly if they really own their mission. When change is proposed without reference to mission, people tend to believe that it's just a pet project or self-aggrandizement of leaders, and they resent the change.

❖ Overcommunicate. People should learn of an innovation under consideration long before it comes to pass. Communicating early and often, and soliciting feedback, will help the group implementing the change to make everyone aware of what they are committing to. One benefit is that someone's feedback will likely point up a potential issue that should be analyzed. Communicating will also help bystanders get used to the idea. When the change finally happens, some people will just be glad there are no more announcements about it!

One of the most effective change mechanisms we've used in Albuquerque is the special edition newsletter. This one-topic, in-depth newsletter comes out on rare occasions, separately from the regular newsletter. Topics have included a history of the issue, a reason for change, what has been considered, a description of the proposed change, how to give feedback, anticipated benefits, and the decision-making process. We've found that we can communicate even complex issues on two sides of an 8.5 × 14-inch newsletter. The newsletter is sent to every household, so it's more likely to be read than any other form of communication, including the regular newsletter.

❖ When implementing a new idea, strive to make as few "losers" as possible. That usually means adding rather than subtracting programs and ministries. Add programs actively; let ineffective programs die on their own.

❖ Attend carefully to the losers in a change, but unless there are a lot of them, count only the yes votes. If there are enough volunteers, money, and participants for a new program, it doesn't matter that most of the people of the church think the program is unnecessary.

❖ When change affects everyone (a change in the congregation's main weekly worship service, for example), do it as an experiment for a stated period of time, say six to twelve weeks, and then take input and make a decision. Most people don't like change until they get used to it. (Remember: l-o-s-s.) If they know they will get their chance to give input, they might tolerate change long enough to come to like it.

❖ Teach and preach that life is change and that accepting change with grace is a hallmark of the mature life. Do so when no particular change in the congregation's life is in the works.

❖ Solicit feedback early and often, and make visible changes in response. People who are invited to give feedback are much less cranky about participating in change. When they are asked to give feedback, many will be responsible enough to actually read and listen to the details of the project, and might make good suggestions for improvement. Finally, feedback gives a leader the opportunity to make public changes in plans. When people learn to trust that their leader is humble enough to change course when necessary, they become, in the long run, more trusting followers and more capable of change.

❖ Remember the wisdom of the Tao: "When the true leader leads, the people say, 'We did this all by ourselves!'" Mature leaders don't need credit for their ideas or for the background work they do to manage change. Satisfaction, not glory, is their reward.

❖ Remember another aspect of the wisdom of the Tao: You can't push the river. When the time is right and the way is prepared, the group will move. A leader who has to yell, cajole, shame, and storm to manage innovation is pushing too hard and may even be pushing the wrong change.

❖ Expect resistance and meet it with listening ears and a compassionate heart. You may not be able to do anything about displacing Mr. Jones from the spot he had sat in for thirty years when you moved pews in your sanctuary. Listen to his sense of loss. When he has been heard with love and thanked for his contribution to the congregation's mission, he is likely to feel better.

❖ Watch the pace of change. People can take in only so much. Don't make a major change in the worship service the same month you ask members to read the newsletter online. The year of economic downturn and other major social change might not be the time to propose a completely different way to do fundraising.

Innovation and church may seem like uneasy bedfellows, but congregations are changing entities in a changing landscape, and if they don't turn to innovation, they will be the victims of change rather than the innovators of new ways to fulfill their mission.

POWER

MARILYN SEWELL

Some native citizens of Northern Rhodesia, using Gandhi's teachings of nonviolent resistance as their guide to counter British imperialism in the mid-20th century, refused to cooperate with the colonial government. The British colonists, on the other hand, were wary of living in a country where their presence was not supported. After putting up with this resistance for several months, the British government sent a new, particularly tough administrator to the colony, a disciplined man who would surely bring these recalcitrant Africans in line. However, when the new administrator arrived at the Lusaka airport, a surprise awaited him. Julia Chikamonenga had organized a group of the biggest women she could find to welcome their new ruler. As he got off the plane, he saw before him a vast sea of naked Zambian women, singing songs of greeting. He turned tail and ordered the pilot to fly, posthaste, back to London.

This story, recounted by Vern Huffman in *The Impossible Will Take a Little While*, is about power and the misuse of power. Colonialism never has moral grounding because it is exploitation based on military and economic superiority. But the story is about another kind of power—the power of people who just said no, who would not cooperate with their oppressors. And it is about using native ingenuity and humor—the informal power of the people—to turn the tables on the formal power of the colonizer. These women, who seemed to have so little worldly power, pulled a kind of aikido move on the British.

Power is exercised by all human beings. Early on, we learn to leverage our gifts to gain advantage of one kind or another. And there are all kinds of power. Some people have great intellectual power, others charisma, others good looks, and still others wealth or charm or talent. Some hold high office, some are physically strong, and others have family ties or reputation. Still others can draw sympathy or attention by their very neediness. In and of itself, power is neither good nor evil: It is morally neutral. It can be used for nefarious ends, or it can be used to heal and to bring justice. The direction it takes depends on the spiritual maturity of the one who wields the power, and the purpose for which it is used.

So if power per se is not evil, why do we fear it in others and, for many, in ourselves? Perhaps we believe Lord Acton's dictum that "power corrupts, and absolute power corrupts absolutely." It is true that great power begets great temptation to disregard or to misuse those who are subject to it. We have ample justification for our fears, given the terrible misuses of power that we have recently witnessed. We saw an administration in Washington that for eight years abused power by starting an illegal war, condoning torture, constraining civil rights. We have seen the Catholic Church shamed because of priests who used the power of their office to molest children, while the church administration looked the other way. We have seen business executives allow their greed and carelessness to bring about untold economic hardship for millions of citizens.

So, yes, we have reason to be fearful. We may have seen ourselves misuse power as we discipline our children or as we speak in a certain tone to our employees. And we are wary of parties who hold power of any kind over us, rightfully doubting that they will use their power well. And yet when our distrust of power makes us reluctant to become powerful and to exercise our power, much is lost to the world.

Let us examine the term more closely. Power is not acting so much as it is the potential or the possibility of acting. The word *power* comes from the Latin *potere*, meaning "to be able." If one is powerful, then, one is potent. When we look at the Indo-European roots of the word, however, we find the root word *poti*, meaning "master" or "lord"; from the Greek, *posis* means "husband." And so the element of dominance or control begins to rear its ugly head. Feminists have most consistently questioned the idea of dominance in relationships. Feminist Riane Eisler, the director of the Center for Partnership Studies, considers the "partnership society" as opposed to the "dominance model" of the patriarchy. James Hillman, in his book *Kinds of Power*, asks, Can we act and exercise power without onerous domination? An adjunct question is whether or not we should do away with hierarchy in our organizational life.

I am a feminist. I want women to be unafraid of their power and to contribute more fully to the political, academic, clerical, and business life of our nation. Being both a mother and the senior minister of a large church has taught me that exercising power and control—parental and organizational—is not only acceptable but essential in order to accomplish certain ends. Hierarchy is the only workable way to structure large organizations.

Let's define some terms before we go further. Definition is important, because it is generally the connotation of certain words rather than the denotation that concerns us. By *dominance*, I mean "to exert the determining or guiding influence." Further, dominate means "to have, or to exert mastery." Guiding or exerting mastery is what leaders do. They do not, as one lay leader explained to me, "put a leash on the big dog, and then follow where that dog pulls you." The "dog" might pull you, for example, to California's Proposition 8, effectively removing civil rights from gays and lesbians, or in earlier days, into a lynch mob. Leaders have vision, and they often go against the grain. They must see beyond what is to what could and must be.

Let us also consider the word *control*. To say that someone has "a controlling personality" is not a compliment. Yet we all admire people who can take control of a situation when necessary. We know that the absence of crowd control can bring chaos and even death. We're familiar with the situation in which the passive facilitator of a question-answer session allows audience members to drone on with lengthy comments, ignoring the needs of the group. "Why doesn't the leader take control?" we wonder. *Control* simply means "the power or authority to manage." We want our current president, for example, to have a strong sense of control and the ability to manage all the forces coming at him. Having control, however, does not mean that he should ignore the views of others, fail to be respectful, or be unwilling to learn and change his mind. But he best be in control of his staff, else his staff will be in control of him, as Dick Cheney was of former President George W. Bush.

I am advocating for leadership, particularly for leadership grounded in a formal structure so that everyone in the organization knows who is responsible for what and who is accountable to whom. I have seen feminist friends try to level everyone in an organization— that is, to make everybody an equal in decision making. In one organization, a law firm, everyone had an equal say, and everyone was paid the same amount, including the secretaries and file clerks. The firm soon dissolved into chaos; moreover, the professionals could not bring in enough money to make payroll. In another example, three female friends opened a law firm in which all were to have an equal voice. Within a year, the firm had broken up, and the most capable lawyer had started her own firm. The third example was a nonprofit: Three feminists convinced the board that they would run the organization as codirectors. Within a year, all three were looking for new jobs. In each of these organizations, no single person was in charge, and there was no clear system of accountability.

The counterpart holds true in the institutional life of churches. I have seen one too many ministers calling themselves "co-ministers" when they were not equal in responsibility nor in salary, making the title misleading and confusing, and ultimately causing conflict and sometimes untimely resignations. I have seen senior ministers struggle when other ministers in the church or even staff members were not accountable to them.

When organizational structure is formal and clear, communication flows easily, questions are answered readily, and responsibility is taken. On the other hand, when leadership of an organization is ambiguous, the result is confusion about responsibilities and bottlenecking around decision making. There is no such thing as a "leaderless group," for if there is no assigned or elected leader, an informal leader will emerge. Then, because power structures are unclear, power will be exercised in covert ways instead of openly by people who are accountable for decisions.

In terms of power structures, then, we should distinguish between those schemes that operate with clarity, efficiency, and responsibility, thereby serving the mission of the organization, and those that repress the contributions and creativity of the many because of the leader's fears or unhealthy ego needs.

People who actively seek power because they are fearful and insecure are the least able to handle it well. Spiritually mature leaders are eager not only to move the mission of the organization forward, but also to give every opportunity for everyone on the team to develop to their fullest potential. To exercise power requires self-confidence, or ego strength. The only question is whether the individual is acting chiefly from ego needs or is in service to something greater. Power colored by ambition, tyranny, selfishness, and greed should be resisted. Power used in the service of others should be honored and upheld.

I went to seminary at Starr King School for the Ministry in the 1980s, and during that period, we still had what were known as "donrags," or individual student meetings with the core faculty twice a year, to evaluate progress and glean advice for continuing study. I had such a meeting just before I was to apply for an internship in a church. I was unencumbered and free to go anywhere in the country—but where to go? I asked the faculty what they thought. They in turn asked me, "What do you want from an internship?" And I answered, "I want to learn how to use power well." They looked at one another, nodded, and all agreed: "Go to Dallas and intern with John Buehrens."

It was a good choice for me. While I was in Dallas the next year, John made the difficult decision to go to New York and minister with Forrest Church at All Souls. We remained close friends, and I supported him in his decision several years later to run for the presidency of the Unitarian Universalist Association. Throughout John's ministry, I saw a man who constantly asked himself, "What am I called to do?" He is a brilliant man, and confident—but he is also clear that his life is about servanthood. He now serves a small church in New England, staying close at hand to his elderly parents. Ministry is about service. Ministers learn early on, "It's not about me." That's the core lesson I got from John. At the same time, ministry is about owning your power and using that power well. That I also learned from John.

But what I saw when I became a minister is that Unitarian Universalists as a group are ambivalent about power. We distrust it. Our ambivalence is understandable, since we're small and we've been ridiculed and persecuted since the very beginning. Some of our forebears in the radical Reformation got themselves burned at the stake by the powers that be. Some people still refer to us as a cult, and we are fodder for many a joke on *Prairie Home Companion*. We have learned to think of ourselves as small and elite rather than large and powerful—*I mean, look at those evangelicals; we wouldn't want to proselytize like they do, would we?*

Many of our Unitarian Universalist churches have little sense of mission, little sense of what the larger world needs. We close in upon ourselves too often and serve mainly the needs of the membership. A visitor shows up on Sunday and hears acronyms which have no meaning to her—GA or UUSC, for example. The visitor commonly hears only first names during the joys and concerns portion of the worship service. *After all, doesn't everyone know Sue?* When a church is self-referential, one must question the "why" of its existence. Is it primarily a club—a place where good friends gather to talk about issues and have potluck dinners? Or is it a church, whose purpose is redemptive in a broken and hurting world? Its power comes directly out of its sense of mission and the spiritual maturity and commitment of its people.

Ours is a free faith, and that is what makes us unique as a religious people. No religious tradition, no book or scripture, no priest or prophet or minister, no authority is predominant over the conscience of the individual believer. Unitarian Universalists understand that theologically, no one can really be anywhere except where he is at any given time.

But there is a shadow side to our freedom of belief. Institutionally, that shadow emerges in our discomfort with authority. In fact, one of our favorite bumper stickers reads, "Question Authority." We attract highly intelligent people with strongly held opinions, many of whom find it difficult to play in an orchestra, so to speak—they are likely more comfortable as soloists. The problem is that, in order to build a well-functioning community and a strong institution, we must pay close attention to structure and leadership.

One of our supreme values as Unitarian Universalists is democratic process and respect for the individual. But "democratic" does not mean that everyone should have the same amount of organizational power nor an equal influence in decision making. Everybody has a voice and a vote, that's all. Respect for the individual does not imply that all individuals are equally wise and capable of leadership. Church groups frequently ask for volunteers for significant positions of leadership, rather than identifying, supporting, and training leaders, a sure formula for inefficiency and dysfunction in an organization.

The term hierarchy has a strong negative connotation these days in Unitarian Universalist circles, because of its association with economic or social class. No Unitarian Universalist should support a hierarchy of value. Our First Principle says it well: Everyone has inherent worth and dignity, and "inherent" is not subject to conditions of wealth or happenstance of birth. But when hierarchy refers to the order and discipline of an organization, it takes on positive value, because such an arrangement ensures that the mission will be clearly focused upon and carried out.

Is structuring an organization hierarchically, although efficient, potentially disrespectful of individuals? The organization might take on a machinelike character, becoming soulless and inhuman. Perhaps tasks get done, but the individuals carrying out the tasks may become expendable, like soldiers during war. Preferable to a rigid, cold hierarchy is one that is flexible, sensitive, and caring. Just because an organization is orderly does not mean that it is heartless.

In fact, order protects not only the mission but also the weaker members of the organization.

Fear and distrust of authority is particularly problematic when it adversely affects the relationship of the congregants to their minister. As pastor, preacher, and institutional leader, the professional minister works with lay leaders to keep the church focused on mission, guiding and supporting them in carrying out that mission. The relationship is contractual—the minister is paid for services rendered—but that contract is wholly subordinate to the convenantal relationship, which is a sacred partnership grounded in love and trust. In many of our churches, lay leaders have patterned their relationship with their minister after the model of the federal government, with its checks and balances of power, resulting in an adversarial relationship rather than a covenantal one. The former is grounded in distrust and assumes bad faith; the latter is one of trust, in which power is freely shared and enhanced.

Power is not limited so that if I have some, you have less. All parties can empower one another as we use our gifts for the good. So functioning effectively as a leader, whether ordained or lay, requires the congregation's trust and support. When the laity do not covenant together to support one another and the minister, the church strains under the stress of power struggles and ends up neglecting its mission. It becomes self-marginalizing in a day and age when our values have never been needed more.

A church is, of course, a special kind of organization. It is not a business, and it is not a nonprofit or a charity. A church should be grounded in theological principle and in spiritual practice. When working with volunteers in a church, for example, we must understand that the quality of the relationships of the people involved is more important than accomplishing the task. That is to say, treating people respectfully is paramount. The ends never justify the means. Needy individuals, however, should not be allowed to dominate groups and meetings. Strong leaders, lay and professional, protect the community from unhealthy individuals. When the community is being threatened or weakened by such people—and every church has them—these leaders will be kind but firm, ensuring that the larger community will not suffer. Our deference to the underdog in Unitarian Universalism comes out of our commitment to justice, I expect, but it does not follow that the weakest members of the community should be allowed to set the agenda.

In churches that have a minister and a staff, the minister—not the board—must be given the responsibility for supervision of the staff, which is not always the case in Unitarian Universalist churches. The board cannot be responsible for supervising staff members, because a body of people cannot function efficiently as a supervisor, and because the board is not there for the day-to-day workings of the church. But, more important, the minister should not be given the responsibility for carrying out policies and programs without the authority to hold the staff accountable. My advice to any minister in search would be to never accept a call to a church in which the board supervises the staff. Responsibility without authority is a recipe for frustration for the minister and dysfunction for the institution.

The Unitarian Universalist model for organization is the town hall meeting of the New England church, where our movement began in this country. But when a church becomes larger than 200 members, this kind of organization doesn't work. The Unitarian Universalist Association has only forty-five large churches, and large for us isn't all that large—only 550 or more adult members.

According to church development books, churchgoers and seekers want large, full-service churches. We know that large churches, with their numbers and resources, can provide a stronger witness in the community than a small church. The small church will always have a place, but why do we have such a preponderance of small churches and so few large ones? One reason is that a church will limit its growth unless it has an appropriate governance system for its size.

Unitarian Universalists are used to the model of a small church, where democracy means that everyone chimes in on every issue. As a result, many churches find it difficult as they grow larger to move to a policy governance model, in which the board, in cooperation with ministry, sets the vision and the goals, and the ministers and the staff carry out those goals. Some version of this model is the only way for a large church to function efficiently. The day-to-day workings of such a church are led by the senior minister, or by an executive team, which can be composed of the senior minister, plus a layperson, an administrator, a financial officer, an associate minister, and others, although it's generally limited to two or three people. In churches with an executive team, however, the leader of that team, in practice if not in fact, is the senior minister. Inevitably, some congregants will fear giving away too much power to the minister. But the minister is accountable always to the board for carrying out the policies and the goals they have set. In addition, the board has legal and fiduciary responsibility for the church, and can and should hold the minister accountable for the responsible, respectful, and mature use of power.

In a staff structure, team players at all levels can and should be respected. The wise leader—the minister, in this case—understands that when one individual on the team is hurting or is weak, the whole team is affected, and will move to support that individual. Leaders should communicate with staff members, for problems are best solved when leaders know what staffers think, how they feel, and what their needs are. A good leader tries to make sure staff members are challenged, giving them opportunities for advancement in the organization, or steering them toward opportunities beyond what the institution can offer.

If it is true that Unitarian Universalist congregations do not wish to be powerful, influential institutions, it is also true that many Unitarian Universalist ministers are unwilling or unable to own their own power, and to lead accordingly. This lack of strong leadership may come from a false egalitarianism or a lack of understanding by laity and ministers alike of the particular power that ordained ministers hold, a power that is different in kind from that of lay leadership.

In short, there is a kind of fear of the holy that may be the chief culprit in much of our movement's powerlessness. We are afraid to be "too religious." Hoping to offend no one, we shrink from religious language and end up with verbiage that loses all force and specificity. We avoid our Judeo-Christian roots, while borrowing copiously from other religious traditions that are far from our cultural moorings and our history. We don't give generously to our churches, compared to adherents of other faiths. In terms of theology, many of our houses of worship are architecturally neutral. Even worse, our places of worship are too often untidy and poorly maintained. If indeed Unitarian Universalists are afraid of getting too close to this realm of the sacred, then it would follow that lay members would try to minimize the "specialness" of their minister and try to dilute the minister's power. And for fear of being perceived as overbearing or controlling, ministers may pull back from exercising the power that was bestowed upon them at ordination. Of late, many congregations have carried out the ritual of the laying on of hands during the ordination service. By asking all of the members of the church to "lay on hands," the congregation suggests that the priestly function is passed to the ordinand through the congregants, rather than through other ministers. I believe that this shift in tradition represents a diminishing of the unique role of the parish minister.

A minister out of touch with his unique role may conclude that he is more a facilitator than leader, more a pastoral friend than one who comes to every encounter not only as the fragile human being that he is, but as a representative of the Holy. Ministers are different from laity. We are set apart. We need to step into the role, understandably fearful of the responsibility, with the faith that led us into the ministry in the first place.

One of my colleagues said that the minister must be willing to be a "fierce shepherd" of the flock. I take this to mean that we must protect our people from the wolves that would destroy community or cripple the institution; we must guard against ethical sloppiness, both in ourselves and in the parish; we must be willing to say no to the board when no is the only answer we can give, even if our position means that we need to resign from the church. We must stand ready to go, if necessary. Some compromises can be made; others cannot.

Laity will respect and follow a minister's leadership more readily if that minister is clear and self-differentiated—even if the lay leaders disagree with the minister's position from time to time, as of course they will. Lay leaders want a strong, spiritually grounded minister who is unafraid of leading boldly. Such a leader will also be closely in touch with the flock, with the signs of the time, and with the needs of the institution. But to pastor is not enough: lead, we must.

When you own your own power, you encourage others to own theirs. Far from keeping others from power, you invite others into power. Some people will be intimidated by leaders who stand in their own power. Those fearful folks will throw stones from the sidelines, because they will not—for whatever reason—be able to accept the invitation into a larger life. But owning power—if it is given to the larger good—is the spiritually healthy way to go. When a minister accepts that challenge, steps faithfully into appropriate power, and leads with strength and love, power will be greatly multiplied. Then all the body of people are likely to be blessed, and in turn, are likely to use their power to bless the world.

People are attracted to health, both in others and in institutions. They are naturally drawn to a church that manifests integrity and spiritual health. Growth comes not from technique or friendly behavior but from the visitor's sense that this institution is strong and safe and devoted to mission.

A visitor enters a church, checking it out. She is looking for a church home, having just moved to the city. Or having just moved out of a marriage. Or having just lost her job. Or having decided that the world is too much with her, and that she needs a spiritual home. A variety of reasons may compel her to return to that church, and decide to stay, but in terms of institutional integrity, she is more likely to return if:

❖ ministers and laity have a deep understanding that their mission is larger than their own personal needs, and they have been empowered to carry out that mission,

❖ leadership, both ministerial and lay, is skilled and respected,

❖ the minister and the laity show that they have a trusting, covenantal relationship,

❖ roles and responsibilities of ministry, staff, board, committee chairs, and other lay volunteers are delineated and clear,

❖ power structures are transparent, and people are accountable, at every level, for their actions,

❖ troubled individuals are integrated into the congregation but are not allowed to dominate the church conversation or to set policy, and

❖ the church identifies boldly as a religious institution, grounded in the spiritual, rather than as a social-political gathering place, which uses amorphous language and a theology designed principally to avoid offending.

Strong church leaders, both professional and lay, will be highly individuated persons who are not afraid to stand in their own truth. They will be open to hearing opinions that differ from their own. They will not operate from self-centered ego needs but from a desire to give their gifts. They will know that the institution must be protected from needy and troubled individuals, and they will watch out for the overall health of the institution. Because they own their power, they will not be afraid of the power of others—in fact, they will call forth the power of others. And because they know themselves and feel their strength, they can lead with love and compassion, out of a spiritual foundation.

The Unitarian Universalist movement throughout its history has embodied values like freedom, love of truth, and devotion to egalitarianism and social progress. But claiming values and actually making those values operative in the world are two different things. Too often we have talked well but have failed to act responsibly.

There is no reason that Unitarian Universalists should not have a stronger voice in the public discourse in the present hour. We need not fear our own power—we need only fear failing to use our power well, and thereby failing to leave this world in a viable condition for our children and our children's children. It's the very least we can do.

LOVE

ELIZABETH LERNER MACLAY

There's a well-known remark near the end of the movie *Jerry Maguire*. As Tom Cruise tries to win back Renée Zellweger with an awkward, impassioned speech about what she means to him, she breaks in, saying, "Just shut up. You had me at 'hello.'"

That's pretty much how I've felt about the UU Church of Silver Spring. Their "hello" was an exceptional letter in their search packet. Here is a slightly abridged version, so you can judge for yourself:

Fall, 2000

Dear Prospective Candidate:

This packet represents the effort of the entire congregation of the Unitarian Universalist Church of Silver Spring to convince you to join us and be our minister. This letter is my one personal opportunity to persuade you that we are a unique and special community, and that your career will blossom at UUCSS as it might nowhere else.

If you are in search of a professional placement, you will receive a number of packets like ours, full of extensive data and an equal anxiety to portray themselves as unique and special. I intend to yield nothing to those other churches who are our competition: UUCSS is every bit as unique and special as they are, and maybe more so. But unique congregations are sort of the hallmark of Unitarian-Universalist churches, aren't they? It is all part and parcel of our being a religion of mavericks.

In truth, I myself did not come to UUCSS because it is unique—just the opposite, in fact. I had been out in the world a long time, going to and fro and walking up and down on it, and my critical senses were well developed. I found that the music at UUCSS was terrific, but also that I remembered the hymns. The worship services were, and continue to be, varied and intellectually stimulating, but also reassuringly familiar. Our people were, and are, a menagerie of brilliant eccentrics—and also warm and welcoming souls, espousing and embodying the values I was raised with. Gradually, I discovered that I, like Frost's hired hand, was ready to come home.

That experience is really what I hope for you: that our packet will intrigue you to the point that you will want to know more, and that, as you understand our advantages and match them to your ambitions, and as you perceive our problems and match them to your abilities, fully as warily and carefully as is fitting for a professional, you will develop a visceral sense that you belong with us.

If that should happen, please come home.

Sincerely,

Larry McAneny

Chairperson, UUCSS Ministerial Search Committee

They had me at "please come home." I still get misty-eyed when I read it.

I've never been much of a believer in love at first sight—but I am a believer in love at first speech. Speech reveals character. The Silver Spring search committee knew they were taking a chance writing such an unconventional cover letter, and it spoke volumes to me in a unique way. Falling in love with the UU Church of Silver Spring was about falling in love with what they said and how they said it, first in that letter and then in their questions and answers and jokes and concerns in each ensuing step through candidating week. When they offered me their ministry, accepting was easy and joyful.

When I looked at them in those early, evaluating days, what I saw was a group of capable people who were intelligent, kind, fun and funny, caring, committed, and hopeful. They were appealing as individuals and as a whole. I saw a strong church with lots of potential to be more. I wasn't sure what that "more" would be—indeed, I couldn't have predicted the directions we eventually took and the ways we changed and grew—but I was sure they would go somewhere and that I wanted to take that journey with them.

In the beginning, I waited for the infamous "end of the honeymoon" phase, when they would see my ugly feet of clay, and I would see their ugly feet of clay, and we would all agree that we had ugly feet and start dealing with it. One year passed, two years—I kept waiting. It has never happened, at least not with the jolt I had been warned to expect. To the contrary, when I look back on almost ten years with them, what stands out is that over and over, they have made me fall in love with them again. I asked a parishioner if she thought the honeymoon was over, and she said yes, because the relationship is not based on unrealistic infatuation but is strong and grounded. As in any good relationship, people are happy to be together and have each other in their lives, and the inevitable feet of clay are vastly outweighed by the good we find in each other.

So what do these mutual positive feelings mean to congregations and leaders, or for our movement as a whole? Perhaps the most important outcome is that love—and the trust and energy that follow— creates an environment in which growth and change are possible. Without that emotional dynamic, congregations can get caught up in other draining dynamics and processes, such as internal struggle, dissatisfaction, and pettiness that divert the energy required for growth and change. Churches, then, need to call ministers they are deeply excited about, who resonate powerfully and quickly inspire affection and trust. "Good enough" is maybe not good enough after all for a congregation that wants serious revitalization and growth. Likewise, ministers who want to serve churches that will grow and change in significant ways need to hold out for compelling parishes, not just those that are convenient or within a good school system. Congregations and ministers that simply want to do church well and are not concerned about working for real growth and change might not be interested. But congregations and ministers excited about those prospects need to build serious, exciting love into the equation.

This emotional dynamic must be present not only for change and growth to thrive but also because change and growth are exhausting. They're hard and challenging for everyone—program and support staff, lay leaders and congregants. They take a long time and must be sustained to effect a lasting, worthwhile impact. But the work itself is imperative: Seminars on healthy churches tell us that a static congregation can't last. In the end, it's either grow and change, or decline and eventually die.

Making hard and courageous choices is inspiring and renewing in itself. Those times when the congregation has renewed my love for and inspiration by them were pivotal times, when they were deciding whether to take a step forward or not. If we believe—and I do—the conventional wisdom about the implications of not changing and growing, then the choice of whether to take a step forward is a big deal. Silver Spring made healthy and brave choices. They chose to try hard things, to make costly commitments, to hold to high standards. Time and again in an annual meeting, the path they chose was impressive, not mundane and not easy to achieve. They'd started an expensive deaf ministry; committed to fairly compensate employees; chosen to offer two services, despite an unsuccessful transition in their past; repeatedly increased church staff hours and positions over the years; and become a multiracial, multicultural congregation. Explicitly riding on those choices was our ability to serve our continually growing community. But implicitly riding on those choices was their trust in me, and in themselves, and their commitment to our community, our values, our faith, and our larger movement. Seeing those commitments powerfully affirmed and reaffirmed is compelling to me as their minister. Despite the tiring challenges of growth, often I leave work for home with a renewed sense of how blessed I am in this remarkable group of people. Lay leaders, take note: This appreciation lifts any minister lucky enough to serve such a congregation.

But it's not all about the big meetings and big decisions. Sometimes it's about the one-on-one conversations, the quick exchanges in the hallway, the note in my mailbox. Sometimes it's about watching someone dig in and do a big task really well, simply because they care that much for our church and our faith. Indeed, some of the moments that mean the most are the efforts the minister observes from a distance, confirming that we are not always needed. That wonderful recognition makes it possible for ministers to last in a settlement. It is a hallmark of a capable, gifted church.

The minister's perception of the congregation might matter more than we realize, although congregations with a strong sense of self can endure a minister's doubts about them. But Silver Spring was a different case when I arrived. They were hurting. Following an unsuccessful period with their previous settled minister, they'd lost many members and pledges, and if that trend had continued much longer, they would have had trouble paying the mortgage payments on their new building. Some congregants doubted themselves as a congregation and as a whole they had an uneven reputation with the larger movement.

Learning about those difficulties raised the question: Were they really the church I'd assumed on the basis of their search letter, or was I making a big mistake? I was surprised at how sure I felt about them, despite their challenging history. From my current vantage point, I wonder: Were they already that church I believed in, or did they become that church because I told them what I saw in them? Did telling them with such conviction enable them to become that church by inviting them into a reality that hadn't otherwise existed?

You can't change people radically just by saying you see them differently and talking them into that different vision. But you can perhaps change them subtly—if the only difference between your vision and their reality is their confidence in and appreciation of who they are. If those are the missing pieces, perhaps the question of whether they are as we see them is moot. The vision of the loving, and faithful, eye is always a true one.

I don't have facts and figures to back that supposition, but I have my experience. In the end, this story is, for me, about the transformative power of love. The phrase is so trite that I didn't take it seriously for a long time; I knew too many stories that told that love itself is not enough. After all, as they say in therapy, people have to want to change. But my experience of partnering with Silver Spring as their minister has added a coda to that truth.

The desire to change is sometimes not enough. Sometimes the catalyst is love, as true for congregations as for individuals. A minister can love a church, see them truly and richly, and through sharing that vision, nudge and inspire the congregation to live up to its best self—a self that is always immanent, such that all it takes is the nudge of the minister's vision to tip them into that existence. Love is critical in this equation—the minister's vision, grounded in love, is something the congregation can perceive and receive. You can't fake it. You can't talk yourself into it. It isn't an idea or a skill you can train for. This feeling must be genuine, a connection that becomes commitment, and even, at the start, an infatuation resulting from a letter, a phrase uttered, the spark in a spirit, the sense of wonderful possibility, of what you might do and be together. Love transforms and lifts us. It's the essence of life.

And love is reciprocally transformative. When UUCSS trusted me and committed themselves to my care, I had to change and grow as they did in order to keep up. Some of that growing and changing has required a lot of learning and effort; some has come naturally and been a pleasure from the start. But the congregation has invited and asked and needed me, as I have them, and the result is that they have fulfilled the audacious promise in their search letter: that my ministry would blossom there as it might nowhere else. Perhaps things would have gone as well in another congregation. But the sense of fitting and momentum, even in challenging times, has been profound and exciting, certainly for me and, I believe, for all of us. This element too requires consideration by every congregation and every minister.

Many of the churches represented at the consultation in Louisville share a similar dynamic of crisis and serious downturn, followed by a significant change (often, but not always, a change in ministers), and then a period of recovery and strong growth. They eventually exceeded previous highs of membership, attendance, programming, and more. Many analysts of institutional growth tell us that a time of crisis is also a time of opportunity. I certainly hope that the changes and engagement necessary for strong growth aren't always triggered by a crisis. But ministers and congregations must remember that the times we feel most challenged are likely the times we need to consider most carefully what is right and necessary to emerge from a crisis best-placed for success.

No doubt, other aspects of ministry and congregational life and leadership are important or essential for significant growth and change. But the question of what the relationship needs to be between minister and church in order to achieve that kind of growth is a new one. Ministering to a growing church is so challenging and exhausting that anything less than love might not sustain a minister through the effort. Perhaps establishing love as another factor for successful growth will help us clarify how essential it is. We might find it's not essential, but I doubt it. All of us who participated in the consultation in Louisville love our churches deeply, love our vocation, and love our larger movement. We believe in them. We are passionate about them.

Many years ago, when I was in seminary, I was told repeatedly that ministry was so hard, the perks and pay so little, that I shouldn't go into it unless there was nothing else I really wanted to do. I didn't believe that then, and with fifteen years of ministry under my belt, I don't believe it now. I would say instead that you shouldn't go into ministry unless you love it, in which case there's nothing else you should do, because there's nothing so rewarding or important. The ministry deserves only people who love it—love ministry, love their congregations, love our movement, all of which deserve nothing less. Love is critical to growth. A congregation must love their minister enough to trust her and endure the challenges that will try their partnership, and a minister must love her congregation in order to serve it well enough to grow.

A Church Growth Inventory

THOM BELOTE

In the previous nine essays, ministers of some of the fastest-growing churches in Unitarian Universalism have shared their thoughts on particular aspects of congregational growth. They have considered concrete and practical facets of growth—excellent worship, a strong welcoming program, and a well-formed mission statement—as well as those more abstract, such as the primacy of love, the feeling of buzz, and an understanding of the effective use of power.

There are three observations that we might make about these essays and about growth in general. First, we could have included reflections on a range of topics that were not addressed at any significant length—essays describing how to achieve growth through excellence in programming, from music to faith development for children and adults, from small group ministry to social action. Their omission does not imply that they aren't important or suggest that they have no bearing on congregational growth. Similarly, we could have included additional writings on topics such as evangelism, marketing, and other ways to grow through public presence.

Second, the essays are by ministers whose churches have grown numerically, but there are other ways that congregations can grow. Loren Mead, author of *More Than Numbers*, writes about growth not only in numerical terms but in terms of *maturational, organic,* and *incarnational growth.* These terms, respectively, refer to the growth of the congregants' faith and spiritual maturity, to the organization's ability to change and adapt, and to the ability of the faith community to proclaim and live out its message in its community and the world. We should not think of numerical growth as in opposition to these other forms of growth. These essays demonstrate that, as our congregations help us "to grow a soul," as A. Powell Davies put it, they will grow in numbers too. When our congregations help us to grow spiritually and theologically, by opening our hearts and putting our faith into action, numerical growth often follows.

Third, there is no magic bean for congregational growth. If there were, somebody would have discovered it and made a lot of money. Differences in aspects of ministry and congregational life do not inhibit growth. A church can grow with a dynamic and charismatic preacher in the pulpit or with a minister whose style is soft and contemplative. A church can grow with a rock band, with classically trained virtuoso musicians, or with authentic and heartfelt musical offerings by amateur musicians who are members of the congregation. A church can grow if its dominant theology is theism or humanism or naturalism.

The examples above demonstrate that growth is not achieved through cookie-cutter approaches to worship, music, governance, or other aspects of congregational life. However, there are certain areas that merit particular attention for congregations that wish to grow. The following questions are designed to encourage reflection about effective leadership that can foster growth.

Would your congregation choose to call a minister who will make or push for changes?

Times of ministerial transition allow congregations to plant important seeds for future growth. When a congregation is in search, the literature it produces about itself will either entice growth-oriented ministers or announce to them that they need not apply.

The search process bears an uncanny resemblance to Internet dating. The records that congregations and ministers post online are similar to the profiles that people post on sites like Match.com.

When I was single, I experimented with Internet dating. Match.com asks its members to answer the question, "What is the last thing you have read?" As an avid reader, I used the answers to this question as a test to determine my initial interest level. But more than the specifics of the books she liked, I knew that my ideal match would be someone who not only had interesting reading habits but also would not downplay her intelligence or shrink from participating in a discussion of ideas.

In the record that congregations create, the equivalent of that question has congregations describe the worst mistake their new minister could make. In the fall of 2002, I entered the search process for my first ministerial call. Since that time, every fall I browse the records of congregations that are in search, not because I am interested in moving on, but because I want to know how they describe what they are looking for in a minister. I always begin by scrolling to the bottom of the pages and reading their answers about the biggest mistake. Obviously, the greatest blunder for any minister would be to commit a felony or engage in unethical behavior, and many congregations offer such an answer. But this doesn't really tell us much, nor does it set a high bar of expectations. The question is not meant to be taken literally. The real question being asked is, "What are you going to clobber your new minister for doing?"

By far, the most common answers to this question over the past seven years are: displaying an authoritarian leadership style, making changes before getting congregational buy-in or permission, and not taking time to understand the culture of the congregation before trying new things. The subtext of these answers is that the congregation is reluctant to grow.

The congregation I serve, the Shawnee Mission Unitarian Universalist Church, answered this question in a way that was so rare as to be singular. Their record read, "The worst mistake that our new minister could make would be to not show enthusiasm and energy in his or her approach to our church, the congregation, and his or her position. We are eager for energy and excitement." This congregation was ready to grow. And it did.

Growth-oriented ministers are not interested in serving congregations that will be resistant to new initiatives or will oppose every new thing they try.

Does your congregation have a covenant that outlines behavioral expectations? Do leaders and members actively engage one another on matters of appropriate conduct and responsible behavior?

Transylvanian Unitarian Francis David offered a powerful affirmation of the potential for religiously pluralistic communities in his succinct statement, "We need not think alike to love alike." Not needing to think alike is an expression of our existence as a faith without a central creed. Loving alike is a nod to the idea of covenant, the understanding that we make deep and significant promises to one another about how we endeavor to be with one another.

As Unitarian Universalists, our congregations are, more often than not, places of acceptance, where good-natured people look for the best in one another. Because our churches are seen as places of intellectual freedom and soul freedom, and because of our heterodoxy and heteropraxy as a faith community, we often attract souls who may not easily fit in many other forms of organized religion. This is good.

When we do not take our covenants seriously, however, we damage the potential for our congregations to grow. Our faith communities are often negligently tolerant of individuals whose behaviors are disruptive or whose conduct detracts from the appeal of our congregations. It is important for congregations to distinguish between being open and being "anything goes." Covenant is something about which members of a congregation need to continually remind one another. Moreover, members share the responsibility for holding one another to their covenant.

A single person whose behavior is disruptive, abrasive, rude, or disrespectful is not capable of impacting a congregation's ability to grow. Rather, it is the system within a congregation that determines whether it will be capable of growth. Put another way, the conduct of one person says very little about the congregation, but the conduct of the group as a whole says a lot. A congregation that appears avoidant of, indifferent toward, or impotent to confront inappropriate conduct is truly off-putting.

Does your congregation clearly articulate expectations for membership? Does it state the desired effects of membership on the lives of its members and measure whether members are achieving them?

One of the most important covenants in any congregation is the covenant of membership. Too many congregations allow their members to define membership for themselves. As a result, membership becomes almost meaningless. Congregational leaders have a responsibility to define membership in a way that makes clear the expectations that come with it. Not doing so is unfair to those trying to figure out exactly what they are getting into when they join a church.

The decision to join a Unitarian Universalist congregation requires careful discernment, which may take some time. Potential members have a right to know exactly what will be expected of them. Insisting on standards is not exclusionary. In fact, a greater clarity about membership helps a church to understand that its programs—worship, learning, and social action, for instance—are more than just "for us."

Does your congregation actively announce its values to the wider community? Is its justice work undertaken consciously and publicly as the manifestation of its faith?

For a long time, I kept a running tally of places that Unitarian Universalists refer to as the buckle of the Bible Belt. I could only conclude that some people wear their pants very high, placing the buckle in Indiana, Illinois, Michigan, or Wisconsin. Others, conforming to a style popularized by today's youth, wear their pants low, placing the buckle in Little Rock, Dallas, or even Houston, giving the impression that one's pants have completely fallen down. More often, the belt buckle is situated in the middle, in such places as Tulsa, Topeka, Louisville, or Nashville. Some seem to insist on wearing their belt buckle to one side (Colorado Springs, for example), whereas others find it fashionable to wear it on the other side (Virginia, the Carolinas, Georgia). Still others seem to accessorize by imagining a buckle not on the Bible Belt but on the Bible shoe (Mississippi, Alabama, and Florida!), or on the shoulder of the Bible handbag (central Pennsylvania), or even on the chin strap of the Bible bicycle helmet (Boise, Idaho). Plotting all of these buckles, I had to conclude that there is no such thing as a Bible Belt. Instead there must be something like a Bible Shroud, with holes cut out for places like the San Francisco Bay Area, Seattle, New York City, and Massachusetts.

Truthfully, I find the term "Bible Belt" offensive. Surely they are not talking about the Bible I read, an inspiring collection of books containing nothing less than a people's battle for liberation, the soothing poetry of the Psalms, the righteous courage of the prophets, and Jesus' good news of inclusive and transformative love.

But when people say "Bible Belt," I hear them expressing a sense of being in the minority and feeling rather alone. This feeling is felt by Unitarian Universalists in all but the places where there is the greatest concentration of our ranks. When referring to congregations in communities where Unitarian Universalists are most likely to feel isolated because of their faith I use the terms "bunker churches" and "beacon churches."

A bunker church faces inward. The outside world is a place that is hostile and dangerous, and a bunker church, taking its cue from 1950s fears of nuclear holocaust, is a place where people hunker down. Members of a bunker church consider it their refuge, their oasis in the middle of the desert, and their bastion of liberal thought. Many people feel this way about their own church—that it is the one place they can go and say what they really think and be who they truly are, without fear. However, cultivating a bunker mentality is antithetical to growth.

In contrast, a beacon church is a community that announces its presence in the community. It boldly proclaims its values, its mission, and its identity. Like a lighthouse, it is visible to those "lost at sea." Like Batman's spotlight, it shows Gotham City that there is a force working for justice, equity, and compassion. It is the little light in the Sermon on the Mount that is not hidden under a bushel basket but is taken out to shine. It is no coincidence that the headquarters of the Unitarian Universalist Association is located on Beacon Street at the top of Beacon Hill. The early Puritans believed that they were to be a light to all the world and took Jesus' words about a city on a hill and not hiding lights under bushel baskets very seriously. Our own Beacon Press published *The Pentagon Papers*. A "Bunker Press" would never do such a thing.

Does your congregation have a relationship with local news outlets? Does it commit news? Is its website up-to-date and designed to appeal to those seeking your congregation?

Connected with the idea of doing ministry publicly is the idea of how to bring attention to your church. A much better way to get the word out than advertising in the newspaper, on the radio (even NPR!), or on television is actually to "commit" news. It turns out to be a whole lot cheaper than advertising. Actually, it turns out to be free.

Making news is a matter of determination and diligence. Press releases can announce all kinds of things: special speakers and community forums, social justice activities, community projects, the arrival of new staff members, the formation of a new activity group, or even a sermon series with a catchy title. News organizations love ideas that appear innovative, unique, edgy, or unconventional. Why should reporters look for news when someone is handing them stories to cover?

To help the congregation grow, it is well worth a minister's time to take a religion editor out to lunch or to make friends with members of the editorial board. Op-ed pieces are great publicity, and news outlets frequently turn to the same sources for quotes and comments, the ones they are familiar with and know to be dependable when it comes to meeting deadlines.

Committing news is the best way to get the attention of those who do not have your congregation on their radar screen. The corollary to this idea is that most of your visitors will tend to be web-savvy people who have done their homework. We've found at the congregation I serve that people come to us already knowing about the seven Principles and the basics of Unitarian Universalism. They are familiar with the staff because they've seen their pictures on our website and have often read several of the sermons that I have published on my blog.

Make sure your website has the information people are seeking. Include the names and pictures of staff; a general summary of Unitarian Universalism; your congregation's mission, vision, and values expressed in a way that is crisp, clear, and catchy; and a description of your worship service. Include a narrative paragraph or a frequently asked questions section, telling people where to park, what door to enter, what the typical dress is, where to go if they have children, and other logistical information.

Does your congregation care for the church as a sacred place? Does its physical space create the impression that this is a place where the holy resides and where transformation happens?

John Buehrens contributed a responsive reading to our hymnal that talks about those "who stay to the end." This reading may seem like a reference to those who are able to last until the end of a committee meeting. However, I think of those who stay until the end of congregational functions to clean up, reset the chairs, and put things back in order. Truly, they are blessed.

I have always felt surprisingly touched by the members who undertake these basic but essential activities: putting things back where they belong after an event, decluttering a space or bringing it to the attention of the facilities staff, taking responsibility for tending plants near the church sign. These simple acts of care, much like the simple yet essential care we invest in our own homes, display a pride in ownership on the part of the members of the congregation.

It is easy to allow spaces in the church to fill up with clutter. It is easy to leave out-of-date information on bulletin boards. It is easy, and often financially expedient in the short term, to delay maintenance on the building. But these behaviors and actions—or inactions—convey a clear message about members' feelings toward their own church community.

Have the leaders in your congregation developed a rhetoric for addressing the anxiety-producing consequences of growth?

Congregations that are growing or that desire to grow take the time to develop a discourse and rhetoric about growth. Their leaders and staff become well versed in theories about the impact of growth on congregational systems and what is necessary to make growth sustainable and healthy.

The church did not begin the moment a member stepped in the door, and will not cease to exist the moment a member leaves. The church has a past, a present, and a future. When I address my congregation about growth, I say that when you first walked into this church, there was a seat in the sanctuary waiting for you. Before you arrived, somebody made sure that there would be an open seat for a person they hadn't even met yet. I then say that it is incumbent upon each member of the church to ensure that there will be an open seat for the next person who walks in, and the next person, and the next.

I try to model healthy ways of addressing the anxiety that change produces in some people, who are distressed to see lots of new faces. When someone comments that "there are too many new people,"

I wonder about the best way to respond. The only "fair" way to solve this problem is to decide what the right number of members is and then hold a lottery—we put everybody's name in a hat and draw the names of those we will kick out of the church so it can return to a comfortable size. Actually, I think there are better ways than this.

I encourage people to make use of their directories. If you see a name that you do not recognize, give that person a call and introduce yourself. Get to know that person. Affinity groups, small-group ministry, and other programs that involve smaller groups of people meeting together are supremely important for giving members the opportunity to feel connected. I frequently make use of the anxiety-diminishing mantra: "This is a great problem to have."

Do leaders in your congregation take the time to learn the literature about growth and change?

Ministers, staff, and leaders must communicate the benefits of growth while addressing the challenges and anxieties it provokes. They must also become well versed in theories of organizational change and the effects that growth has on all parts of a church system. A good place to start is the work of Alice Mann of the Alban Institute, who has written extensively on size transitions in congregations. Gil Rendle has written about navigating change in church life. For those congregations that want to take the next step, the works of Thomas Bandy and Bill Easum offer provocative ideas to congregations trying to make sense of their growth. The "Resources" section at the end of this book contains a host of helpful information.

These suggestions are designed to supplement the essays by my colleagues—to fill in some of the cracks and briefly address some of the areas that were not considered.

With all my colleagues, I share a fundamental faith in the transformative power of Unitarian Universalism in the lives of individuals, families, and the larger world. Each new person who walks through the doors of one of our churches is a blessing and an opportunity for us to share our gifts of ministry. Ours is a faith with the power to save and transform lives, to help people grow in their capacity to love and in their commitment to serve the causes of goodness and healing in this world.

It is too sacred an opportunity for us to miss.

ABOUT THE CONTRIBUTORS

KEN BELDON is the lead minister of WellSprings Congregation in the Greater Philadelphia area. In 2005 he headed the efforts to launch this new congregation from scratch. WellSprings began offering weekly services in 2007 and today has an average Sunday attendance of over 150. Prior to this, he served a congregation in Plantation, Florida.

THOM BELOTE is in his seventh year serving the Shawnee Mission Unitarian Universalist Church in suburban Kansas City. He has recently completed a three-year term on the Executive Committee of the Unitarian Universalist Ministers Association and has presented on congregational growth at various leadership retreats and at General Assembly. He blogs at www.revthom.blogspot.com.

JOHN T. CRESTWELL JR. is associate minister at the Unitarian Universalist Church of Annapolis. He was formerly the minister of Davies Memorial Unitarian Universalist Church, where he assisted in its expansion into a multiracial congregation. Under his leadership, 40 percent of the Davies congregation included people of color. He is author of *Conversations: The Hidden Truth That Keeps the World from Being at Peace* (2001) and *The Charge of the Chalice* (2007), which tells the story of Davies Memorial's growth in racial diversity.

ELIZABETH LERNER MACLAY is the minister of the Unitarian Universalist Church of Silver Spring, Maryland. During her tenure there, the staff has more than doubled in size and the congregation has grown by 60 percent, including a significant increase in its racial and cultural diversity. She has also served congregations in Mt. Kisco, New York, and Lexington, Massachusetts.

ALICE MANN is a senior consultant with the Alban Institute and a leading author on congregational vitality, whose books include *Can Our Church Live? Redeveloping Congregations in Decline; Raising the Roof: The Pastoral to Program Size Transition;* and *Holy Conversations: Strategic Planning as a Spiritual Practice for Congregations.*

PETER MORALES is the president of the UUA. Before beginning his term in 2009, he served as senior minister at Jefferson Unitarian Church in Golden, Colorado. He also served for two years as the UUA's director of district services. Morales is a former member of the UUA Board of Trustees and of the Unitarian Universalist Ministers Association Executive Team.

CHRISTINE ROBINSON has been the minister of First Unitarian in Albuquerque since 1988. During that time, the congregation has nearly doubled in size, has started a new church west of Albuquerque, and has organized three branches of the congregation in Edgewood, Socorro, and Carlsbad, New Mexico. Robinson is co-author of *Heart to Heart: 14 Gatherings for Reflection and Sharing,* a book of resources for small group ministry.

VICTORIA SAFFORD is the minister of White Bear Unitarian Universalist Church in Minnesota, a congregation that has grown three-fold since she started there in 1999. She has also served a congregation in Northampton, Massachusetts. She is the author of the collection of meditations *Walking Toward Morning* (2003) and editor of another such collection, *With or Without Candlelight* (2009).

MICHAEL SCHULER has served the 1,500-member First Unitarian Society of Madison, Wisconsin, for the past twenty-one years. Under his leadership the congregation recently completed a $9 million dollar sustainably designed addition to their Frank Lloyd Wright Meeting House. He is the author of *Making the Good Life Last: Four Keys to Sustainable Living* (2009).

MARILYN SEWELL retired in June 2009 after seventeen years as senior minister of the First Unitarian Church of Portland, Oregon. She has also served congregations in Cincinnati, Ohio, and Napa, California. She is the editor of two books of women's poetry, *Cries of the Spirit* and *Claiming the Spirit Within*, and two volumes of essays, *Resurrecting Grace: Remembering Catholic Childhoods* and *Breaking Free: Women of Spirit at Midlife and Beyond*. Her two most recent publications are *A Little Book on Forgiveness* and *A Little Book on Prayer*.

WILLIAM SINKFORD served as UUA president from 2001 until 2009. He called together the UUA Growth Team and charged it to articulate a vision for the growth of the Association and develop strategies to encourage, inspire, and support that growth. The consultation that led to this book was one of those strategies. Prior to his election as president, he supervised the Association's extension efforts. He currently serves as senior minister and advisor to the Unitarian Universalist Urban Ministry in Roxbury, Massachusetts.

Resources

Wayne Arnason and Kathleen Rolenz, *Worship That Works: Theory and Practice for Unitarian Universalists*, Skinner House, 2007.

Thomas G. Bandy, *Kicking Habits: Welcome Relief for Addicted Churches*, Abingdon, 2000.

_____, *Coaching Change: Breaking Down Resistance, Building Up Hope*, Abingdon, 2000.

_____, *Coming Clean: The Study Guide to Kicking Habits*, Abingdon, 2001.

_____, *Spirited Leadership: Empowering People To Do What Matters*, Chalice Press, 2008.

John Crestwell, *The Charge of the Chalice: The Davies Memorial Unitarian Universalist Growth and Diversity Story*, Movement Ministries, 2007.

Michael Durall, *The Almost Church*, Jenkin Lloyd Jones, 2004.

_____, *The Almost Church Revitalized*, CommonWealth Consulting Group, 2009.

_____, ed., *Living a Call: Ministers and Congregations Together*, Jenkin Lloyd Jones, 2006.

Bill Easum and Thomas G. Bandy, *Growing Spiritual Redwoods*, Abingdon, 1997.

Dan Hotchkiss, *Governance and Ministry: Rethinking Board Leadership*, Alban, 2009.

Barbara Kellerman, *Followership: How Followers Are Creating Change and Changing Leaders*, Harvard Business School, 2008.

Robert T. Latham, *Moving On from Church Folly Lane: The Pastoral to Program Shift*, Wheatmark, 2006.

Tamara Lebak and Bret Lortie, eds., *Reverend X: How Generation X Ministers Are Shaping Unitarian Universalism*, Jenkin Lloyd Jones, 2008.

Listening to Experience: 12 Visionary Ministers Discuss Growth (DVD), UUA, 2008.

Alice Mann, *The In-Between Church: Navigating Size Transitions in Congregations*. Alban, 1998.

_____, *Raising the Roof: The Pastoral-to-Program Size Transition*, Alban, 2001.

Marcia McFee, *The Worship Workshop: Creative Ways to Design Worship Together*, Abingdon, 2002.

Loren B. Mead, *More Than Numbers: The Ways Churches Grow*, Alban, 1993.

Tom Owen-Towle, *Growing a Beloved Community: Twelve Hallmarks of a Healthy Congregation*, Skinner House, 2004.

Gilbert R. Rendle, *Leading Change in the Congregation: Spiritual and Organizational Tools for Leaders*, Alban, 1997.

_____ and Susan Beaumont, *When Moses Meets Aaron: Staffing & Supervision in Large Churches*, Alban, 2007.

_____ and Alice Mann, *Holy Conversations: Strategic Planning as a Spiritual Practice for Congregations*, Alban, 2003.

Michael A. Schuler, *Making the Good Life Last: Four Keys to Sustainable Living*, Berrett-Koehler, 1999.

Marilyn Sewell, *Unitarian Universalist Culture: The Present and the Promise*, Fuller Press, 2007.

UU Planet Growth Resource Page, www.uuplanet.com/resources/growth/index.html